A-4   4-

Processing French

Processing French

a psycholinguistic perspective

PETER GOLATO

University of Illinois at Urbana-Champaign

Yale University Press   New Haven and London

Publisher: Mary Jane Peluso
Editor: Ann-Marie Imbornoni
Editorial Assistant: Brie Kluytenaar
Production Controller: Karen Stickler
Designer: Sonia Shannon
Marketing Manager: Timothy Shea

Set in Minion type by Integrated Publishing Solutions.
Printed in the United States of America.

Library of Congress Cataloging-in-Publication Data
Golato, Peter, 1965–
Processing French : a psycholinguistic perspective / Peter Golato
p.   cm.
Includes bibliographical references and index.
ISBN 0-300-10835-4 (pbk. : alk. paper)
1. French language—Psychological aspects.
2. Psycholinguistics.   I. Title.
PC2073.G57   2006
440'.19—dc22   2005016027

A catalogue record for this book is available from
the British Library.

The paper in this book meets the guidelines for permanence and
durability of the Committee on Production Guidelines for Book
Longevity of the Council on Library Resources.

10 9 8 7 6 5 4 3 2 1

Contents

Acknowledgments

Good ideas are rare and seldom spring forth out of nowhere, while bad ideas seem to abound (in my case, anyway). I take full responsibility for any bad ones that appear in this book, while recognizing that the good ones will inevitably have had their source in the work of others.

I owe a tremendous debt of thanks to those researchers whose collective work inspired me to conduct the studies I offer here. Their work tells a provocative and fascinating story about the mental representation of words and sentences; I fervently hope that I have relayed that story well.

I wish to thank the friends and colleagues who lent me their support as I assembled the empirical portions of this book. I thank the Department of French of the University of Illinois for granting me a semester-long teaching release. I thank David Birdsong for his encouragement as I embarked on this project. I thank Viviane Ruellot for assisting me in subject recruitment and for lending me her voice in the creation of stimulus items. And I am indebted to Jeff Magoto, Dana Raymond, and all the Yamadians of the University of Oregon's Yamada Language Center for their warm hospitality and for graciously allowing me testing space at their facility during the summer of 2003.

I am grateful for the encouraging feedback and comments I have received on presentations of portions of the work described herein. In particular, I thank the audience attending my fall 2003 presentation at the *Fruchtbringende Gesellschaft* of the Department of Germanic Languages and Literatures at the University of Illinois, as well as the attendees of my presentation at the spring 2004 annual conference of the American Association of Applied Linguistics in Portland, Oregon. I also wish to gratefully acknowledge my colleagues Alice Hadley and Douglas Kibbee for reading drafts of the manuscript and for providing invaluable feedback and suggestions for improvement.

I wish to acknowledge Fred Davidson and B. Kumaravadivelu for having agreed to be outside reviewers. I am especially grateful to Fred Davidson for his interest in my project. Among the people at Yale University Press I especially wish to thank are Mary Jane Peluso, for her encouragement and for her confidence in my project, and Annie Imbornoni, for her good humor and for her care and attention in editing my manuscript.

Lastly, I owe my warmest and most sincere thanks to my wife, Andrea, for all that she has been, is, and will be for me. I dedicate this book to her, with love and gratitude.

Processing French

Introduction

Current theories and research on the psychology of word- and sentence-level language processing generally posit two kinds of processes: associative, data-driven processes and symbolic, rule-based processes. Findings from behavioral studies suggest that we understand and produce language using a combination of both kinds of processing. To date, the majority of psycholinguistic evidence for a "dual-mechanism" theoretical perspective comes from word-level studies conducted with Germanic languages. Results from studies testing speakers of non-Germanic languages, however, point to an almost exclusive reliance upon rule-based processes.

This book was written to address two questions. First, can support for the dual-mechanism perspective be obtained using a non-Germanic language such as French, a language for which the findings to date do not support a dual-mechanism account of processing? Second, can behavioral studies simultaneously offer a view onto both word-level and sentence-

level, that is, morphological and syntactic, processing, thereby
providing a new perspective on the processing debate?

A Challenge to Classical Models
of Mind: Connectionism

In 1986, Rumelhart and McClelland and the PDP Research
Group reported that a computer (i.e., artificial intelligence, or
AI) simulation of a neural network had modeled humanlike
performance in its production of significant portions of the
English past tense, and it had even correctly overgeneralized
English past-tense forms from novel items, thereby mimicking
the English past-tense acquisition behavior of infant learners.
Amazingly, Rumelhart and McClelland's connectionist network had managed this feat without having recourse to anything resembling a rule for creating past-tense forms. Instead,
the network had learned to model the English past tense
purely on the basis of extensive training. This report was of
tremendous significance; it challenged the classical view of
mind, according to which all cognition proceeds from the application of algebraic rules that operate upon symbols or variables (see, e.g., Johnson-Laird, 1988; Newell, 1980; Newell and
Simon, 1972; Pylyshyn, 1984). In this case the regular English
past tense, a feature of grammar that has traditionally been described with reference to linguistic rules (i.e., "to form the past
tense of *walk, open,* or any other regular English verb, add *-ed*
to the verb's infinitival form"), had been learned without using
such rules. According to classic, symbolic accounts of cognition, the statement corresponding to the linguistic rule is to be
understood as a high-level description of the mental combinatorial process through which speakers of English compute the
regular past tense. Rumelhart and McClelland's finding called
this account into question; here was an instance of all-or-

nothing, rulelike behavior that did not have its source in a rule. Moreover, Rumelhart and McClelland's connectionist network had done what even Deep Blue could not do when it defeated Garry Kasparov eleven years later: it had learned from its mistakes and adjusted its output accordingly, much as humans do.

A second reason for the significance of Rumelhart and McClelland's report is that their network had also been reasonably successful in coping with semiregular patterns occurring among the English irregular past-tense forms. Thus, faced with irregular verbs with semiregular patterns such as *spring* and *sneak* and similar-sounding regular verbs such as *ding* and *tweak*, the network was often able to produce the correct forms *sprung* and *snuck* and *dinged* and *tweaked*. Purely symbolic accounts would have to posit separate rules for the semiregularities among the irregular verbs. Moreover, only phonological rules of an implausibly baroque nature could capture all the semiregularities. Nevertheless, Rumelhart and McClelland's network was often able to generalize correctly to make novel irregular past-tense forms from the semiregular irregular-verb patterns on which it had been trained, while keeping the novel irregulars separate from similar-sounding regulars, to which the network correctly added the regular past-tense inflection, *-ed*.

The Response to Connectionism: Words and Rules Theory

In response to Rumelhart and McClelland's study, Steven Pinker and colleagues have gradually elaborated a dual-mechanism model of language processing known as words and rules theory. In its most recent iteration (Pinker, 2000; Pinker and Ullman, 2002), it holds that all language processes belong to one of two computational systems: a symbolic, combinatorial module (i.e., a grammar) and a linguistically structured word repository (i.e., a lexicon). With respect to the regular and irregular English past tense (e.g., *walked* vs. *went*, respectively), words and rules theory is thus neither exclusively symbolic nor exclusively associationist but instead posits roles for both kinds of processing. Specifically, the theory asserts that productive word-, phrase-, and sentence-building processes tend to be executed on an as-needed basis by the symbolic module. In contrast, simplex or idiosyncratic linguistic items are stored in and retrieved from the lexicon. In this view, the symbolic module is responsible for the on-the-fly formation of the English regular past tense; the lexicon is responsible for the storage and retrieval of English irregular past tenses.

Although words and rules theory has been supported by linguistic, behavioral, and neuropsychological data from English and German, questions still remain with respect to the scope of the theory. For instance, psycholinguistic support for words and rules theory has been found primarily through studies examining the comprehension or production of isolated words. However, people produce and understand utterances that are longer than single words and that often embody complex syntactic relations. (In mainstream theories of syntax, such relations include traces and various kinds of coreferenced, moved elements.) Although words and rules theory holds that syntactic processing is symbolic, and online studies of sentence processing (that is, studies using tasks that measure changes in sentence processing load in very small time increments) suggest that this is true, there is to date no online behavioral evidence that addresses the nature of the relation between words-and-rules-theory-type word-level processing and sentence-level, syntactic processing. Moreover, the isolated words examined in past studies have often been limited to English infinitives and their inflected forms; few studies, with the notable exception of Harald Clahsen and colleagues' work with German (see, e.g., Clahsen et al., 2001; Clahsen, Sonnenstuhl, and Blevins, 2003), have sought to establish whether the words-rules distinction exists among derived linguistic forms as well. Finally, there have been relatively few studies of non-Germanic languages that have found support for words and rules theory, prompting some researchers (e.g., Marslen-Wilson and Tyler, 1998) to suggest that the regular-irregular basis of words and rules theory might simply reflect idiosyncratic properties of the English past-tense system. Indeed, the results of the published studies that have examined word-level regular-irregular verb contrasts in French (Meunier and Marslen-Wilson, 2000; Meunier and Marslen-Wilson, 2004; Royle, Jarema, and Kehayia, 2002) do not unequivocally support a words-and-rules-theory-type account of language processing.

Outline of This Book

This book reports upon an empirical investigation of the preceding discussion. Using French language items and French native speakers, it contributes to the symbolic- and associative-processing debate through both word- and sentence-level psycholinguistic studies. The book is organized as follows. Chapter 1 will provide an overview of current theories of language processing, with special reference to words and rules theory and connectionist models. The overview will also serve to highlight the rulelike versus idiosyncratic nature of the linguistic items tested in the literature. A review of behavioral studies conducted with English regular and irregular verbs and native speakers of English will reveal that a verb's morphological status (that is, whether the verb is regularly or irregularly inflected) will have the most influence on the manner in which the item is processed.

The preponderance of evidence to date that suggests the relative efficacy of associative and symbol-manipulating theories of language has been collected in the context of online behavioral studies. In many of these studies, participants take part in what appear to be ordinary visual lexical-decision tasks (i.e., a participant must decide whether a string of letters is or is not a word in their language); however, such studies can involve more than what consciously meets the eye. Some of the most exciting findings in language-processing research have been obtained through masked-priming experiments, in which certain visual-stimulus events are presented so rapidly that the participant remains completely unaware of their presence. Nevertheless, research has shown that these subliminal-stimulus events do affect participant performance in online experiments. Accordingly, chapter 2 will review findings from the priming literature in experimental psychology and cognitive science, both generally and with respect to studies investigating word-level regular-irregular verb contrasts in Italian and French, thereby setting the stage for discussion of the primed lexical-decision tasks used in the experiments that constitute the core of this book. Also developed in chapter 2 is the idea that morphological *productivity* (that is, the extent to which a linguistic item such as a suffix has spread in use) is the concept upon which the words-rules distinction turns in French.

Chapters 3–6 will discuss four priming experiments, all of which were conducted with French language items and French native-speaker participants and which were designed to investigate the role of morphological productivity at both the word and the sentence level. More generally, the experiments were designed to explore whether the processing facts they revealed would be more in accordance with the partly symbolic, partly associative words and rules theory or with the exclusively data-driven theory of connectionism.

The two word-level priming experiments examined the real-time comprehension of both inflected verbs and derived (i.e., suffixed) nouns. The two sentence-level priming experiments investigated the real-time processing of inflected verbs and derived nouns within syntactic movement operations, specifically *wh*-movement and lexical verb raising. Taken together, the results of the four experiments suggest that certain noun suffixes in French appear to be "dying out" in that the number of nouns in which they can be found has been steadily decreasing over the last three centuries, while other suffixes have shown increasing evidence of productivity during the same time period. Moreover, the results suggest that these differing patterns of productivity have processing consequences: productively suffixed French nouns bear the behavioral signatures of a rulelike, root-suffix combinatorial process, while unproductively suffixed French nouns do not. Also, in line with a well-supported theory of sentence processing (the trace reactivation account; Nicol and Swinney, 1989), the sentence-level studies point to the psychological reality of syntactic traces (that is, silent, syntactically active "remnants" of displaced sentential elements). The sentence-level studies are innovative in that they also afford a glimpse of the interaction between syntactic and morphological processing in the online context.

In chapter 7, the book discusses the implications of the findings from experiments 1–4 with respect to current theories of language processing. The overall findings are interpreted as supporting words and rules theory. Moreover, it is argued that the results of the two sentence-level experiments also support words and rules theory at the syntactic level. The book concludes with suggestions for further research.

I

Theories of Language Processing

Wugs and *Goed:* Evidence for the Child Acquirer's Use and Overuse of Rules

The basic distinction between morphological regularity and irregularity has figured in child language-acquisition studies since at least the 1950s. For instance, researchers such as Anisfeld and Tucker (1967), Berko (1958), Bryant and Anisfeld (1969), and Ervin (1964) all noted that at a certain point in their linguistic development (roughly between the ages of four and seven), child acquirers of English are able to productively inflect novel verbs with regular past-tense endings and novel nouns with regular plural endings. To take one example, Berko (1958) found that when child acquirers of English were shown a picture of a fictitious animal and told that it was a *wug*, they were able to produce its correct plural form: *wugs*. Since the children in these studies had never heard the word *wug* before (and presumably had never heard its plural form either), the results were taken as evidence that children are able to use a suffixation rule in order to create regular English plural and past-tense forms.

There is further naturalistic evidence that child acquirers of English productively use rules. This evidence comes from documented instances of overgeneralizations of the inflectional endings of the English regular past-tense and plural forms. For example, at about the same time that they become able to productively inflect novel verbs with regular past-tense endings and novel nouns with regular plural endings, children acquiring English will overgeneralize the past-tense suffix -ed both to the root forms of irregular verbs (e.g., *sing-singed*) and to irregular verbs already in the past tense (e.g., *broked;* see, e.g., Anisfeld, 1984; Slobin, 1985). Curiously, these children will have previously produced many of these same past-tense forms correctly. Again, these observations have been interpreted as supporting the notion that children are overapplying rules of inflectional morphology to create ungrammatical yet (apparently) rule-generated English regular past tenses and plurals.

The Status of Regular Morphological Rules in the Adult Mind

Of course, pathologically normal children do eventually retreat from the above-described overgeneralizations (see Marcus et al., 1992, for a discussion of how this might happen). Nevertheless, regular-irregular differences in English past-tense morphology have remained interesting to researchers in cognitive science, linguistics, and psycholinguistics who seek to establish the extent to which differences in the morphological structure of regularly and irregularly inflected items reflect differences in how these forms are represented in the minds of both children and adults.

Generally speaking, there are currently two types of explanation for the acquisitional, distributional, and (as we shall see) processing differences between English regular and irregular past-tense forms. *Single-mechanism* theories hold that both regulars and irregulars are processed—that is, produced and understood by speakers of a language—by a single associative memory system. *Dual-mechanism* theories instead propose that regulars are the product of symbolic, algebraic rules, while irregulars are stored in and retrieved from a partly associative mental lexicon. Below, I present an overview of and supporting evidence for both theoretical perspectives. Mirroring recent cognitive scientific discourse on this topic (see, e.g., Pinker and Ullman, 2002; McClelland and Patterson, 2002), this book will use the theory of *connectionism* to represent the single-mechanism perspective and *words and rules theory* to represent the dual-mechanism perspective.

Example of a Single-Mechanism Theory: Connectionism

As stated above, in this book connectionism (Rumelhart and McClelland, 1986; Elman and McClelland, 1986; Rumelhart, McClelland, and PDP Research Group, 1986; Elman et al., 1996) will represent the single-mechanism perspective. The origins of connectionism lie in research on artificial intelligence (AI), which has been defined as "the branch of computer science that investigates the extent to which the mental powers of human beings can be reproduced by means of machines" (Dunlop and Fetzer, 1993, p. 6). This includes designing machines that will engage in intelligent behavior when made to perform such actions as solving problems, playing chess games, or doing other similar activities.[1] Whatever its purpose, AI research can be classified according to the extent to which it is either strong or weak AI, or to the extent to which it is symbolic (top-down) or connectionist (bottom-up) AI. A strong AI system not only exhibits intelligent behavior but also is sentient or self-aware. Strong AI systems exist only on the silver screen, with one of the more recent (and malevolent) examples being the snappily dressed, pistol-packing Agents of the *Matrix* movie trilogy. If any strong AI systems have in fact been created, either their designers have not gone public with the news, or the strong AI systems themselves have not volunteered evidence of their own existence. By contrast, weak AI systems exhibit intelligent behavior but are not self-aware. Designers of weak AI systems view their creations not as complete models of human consciousness, but as models of ways in which information processing might proceed in the mind. Weak AI systems have been designed that play games, solve problems, or, as we will see below, learn the English past tense. An example of a product of weak AI research would be Deep Blue, the chess-playing computer that defeated Garry Kasparov. While Deep Blue was clearly able to execute chess moves, it was neither aware that it was playing chess nor capable of other recognizably human behaviors.

The other dimension by which AI research may vary is the extent to which it is symbolic or connectionist. Symbolic AI research views human intelligence as emerging from the brain's manipulation of symbols. In this account of human intelligence, these symbols are variables, or placeholders; as such, they do not represent individual instantiations of objects but instead abstract categories according to which the objects or entities in the world have been classified. The symbol manipulations performed by the brain are conceived as being algebraic-like rules. As a result, symbolic AI researchers attempt to model human intelligence by designing AI programs that mirror this view of human cognition. Symbolic AI programs have built-in, higher-order representations of entities and objects as well as representations of classes of entities or objects, and they include rules specifying the possible operations that can be performed upon an entity or an object.

The reason that the symbols and rules of a symbolic AI program must be supplied by the programmer is because such programs have no built-in capacity to learn from their environment. Thus in most cases, these programs cannot ever know anything more about their world than what was built into them; as a result, they typically have neither the capacity to learn new information nor the capacity to learn through making mistakes. Possibly the most difficult obstacle for symbolic AI programs to overcome, however, is representing and implementing the background or commonsense knowledge of the world that all humans acquire and are able to reason with (Dreyfus, 1992). Attempts have been made to overcome this shortcoming of symbolic AI, usually either by carefully limiting the world within which the AI system must function, or by attempting to capture within sufficiently abstract semantic frames or scripts a common core of the seemingly diverse range of situations in daily life. Examples of such attempts include building programs with a tightly constrained, rule-based micro-world such as that found in a chess game (see also, e.g., the block world of SHRDLU; Winograd, 1970) or with real-world knowledge but only of select, highly specific situations (such information is contained within semantic frames, or collections of information about a stereotyped situation such as a restaurant setting, a birthday party, etc.; e.g., Minsky, 1975; see also Schank and Abelson, 1977, for a related script-based approach).

In these and other examples of symbolic AI programs, little concern is shown for modeling actual brain processes. Symbolic AI researchers are usually not concerned with how their programs might acquire the knowledge they have of their microworlds, frames, or scripts; in many cases the symbols and rules used to manipulate them are simply taken as a given and are built into the system from the start.

Connectionist AI, by contrast, seeks to create AI systems that to some degree model the structure and functioning of the human brain and human learning processes themselves. In this view of human intelligence, learning occurs through both supervised and unsupervised interaction with the environment. At its most basic level, this learning is thought to occur in a bottom-up fashion: a flow of simple or low-level information enters the system from the outside world, and as it is processed by the brain, the low-level information is transformed into higher-order representations.

The human brain possesses a staggeringly complex circuitry. A recent study estimates that there are approximately twenty-one billion neurons—the number varies by sex and age—in the adult neocortex (Pakkenberg and Gundersen, 1997). Far more important than the sheer number of neurons, however, is the degree of interconnectivity between them: some estimates have suggested an average of two thousand neuronal connections, or synapses, per neuron (Pakkenberg et al., 2003). This means that on average, the twenty-one billion neurons in an adult's neocortex are networked by forty-two trillion synapses. These neuronal connections can either be excitatory (that is, they cause a neuron to fire, or release chemical neurotransmitters across synaptic gaps to the neurons surrounding it, thereby exciting those neurons to fire as well) or inhibitory (that is, they discourage a neuron from firing). It is thanks to this massive interconnectivity at the cellular level that the brain is able to process and integrate information the way it does.

Thus, connectionist AI researchers attempt to model human intelligence by designing AI programs that mirror our current understanding of how the brain processes information at the cellular level. In contrast to symbolic AI programs, connectionist AI programs usually consist of computational matrices that mimic the networked structure and information flow patterns of interconnected neurons in the brain. One part of the computational matrix represents an array or layer of input neurons, or nodes, while another part represents a layer of output nodes. In recent neural network designs, there may also be a "hidden" layer of nodes between the input and output layers. (They are referred to as hidden because they never have direct contact with the outside world.) As in a real brain, the input and output nodes in an artificial neural network are connected; however, they are not connected physically but mathematically, such that as an input node is turned on (i.e., is told to fire by the program), it sends an excitatory message to the output node(s) it is connected to. Through one of several possible learning algorithms, the network receives feedback during its course of training on the accuracy of its output activations. This feedback is then used to mathematically adjust the strengths of the connections between nodes. In this way, for a given input, connections for correct answers are strengthened while connections for incorrect answers are inhibited. The result is that the network is able to gradually tune itself such that only the correct output is likely to be activated for any particular input.

With respect to efforts to model the acquisition and processing of language, possibly the best known connectionist networks are the parallel distributed processing (PDP) models of Rumelhart and McClelland (Rumelhart, McClelland, and PDP Research Group, 1986). Two terms may require explanation: *parallel* means that processing of input occurs simultaneously throughout the network, and *distributed* means that there is no command center, or central location in the network where executive decisions are made. These models have also been called *pattern associators* in that they associate one kind of pattern (for instance, a pattern of activated input neurons) with another kind of pattern (for instance, a desired pattern of activated output neurons).

Two well-known PDP models have been designed to cope with different aspects of language processing. The first model, McClelland and Ellman's (1986) TRACE model of phoneme perception and lexical access, was a PDP network of detectors and connections arranged in three layers: one of distinctive-feature detectors, one of phoneme detectors, and one of word detectors. The connections between layers were bidirectional and excitatory, meaning that while lower-level information could feed forward to higher-level layers, higher-order information could also percolate back down and thereby influence detection at the lower-level layers. By contrast, the connections within a given layer were inhibitory. In detecting a word or a phoneme, the feature detectors first extracted relevant information from a spectral representation of the speech signal. That information then spread according to the relative strength of activation of certain distinctive-feature detectors over others to the layer of phoneme detectors. In the case of word detections, the phoneme detectors then activated words in the third layer of the network. The bidirectional, excitatory nature of the connections between layers, coupled with the inhibitory nature of the connections within a given layer, conspired to increasingly activate one lexical candidate over all others while simultaneously suppressing competing candidates. Information related to representing the temporal unfolding of a word was modeled by repeating each feature detector multiple times, thereby allowing the possibility of both past and possible upcoming information to be activated along with current information. Using this interactive network architecture, McClelland and Ellman (1986) showed that the TRACE model could successfully simulate a number of phoneme and word detection phenomena that had been observed in experiments with human participants. For example, in phoneme detection experiments, it was observed that factors pertaining to phonetic context (i.e., the phonemes that precede and follow a target phoneme) appeared to aid people in detecting phonemes or in recovering phonemes that had been partially masked with noise.[2] The TRACE model also produced this finding.

In a second simulation, Rumelhart and McClelland (1986) used a pattern associator network to model not speech perception, but the acquisition of the English past-tense system. For this study, the researchers began by noting that although the findings surrounding the acquisition of the English past tense have been interpreted as bearing the hallmarks of rule-based development (with clearly marked and nonoverlapping stages of development), the documented facts (some of which were reviewed above) could also be argued to suggest instead that acquisition proceeds on a less categorical, more gradual basis. To a certain extent, therefore, the observed facts would also appear to be in line with the predictions of a more probabilistically based acquisition account. Thus, one of the goals of Rumelhart and McClelland (1986) was to successfully model this kind of gradual convergence upon the correct forms of the English past tense.

The task facing their pattern associator network was the successful acquisition of 506 (408 regular and 98 irregular) English verbs, which were sorted according to frequency (low, medium, and high). This meant that the same network had to associate both irregular infinitives with their largely idiosyncratic past tenses, and regular infinitives with the regular -ed past tense. In order to have a relatively constrained number of naturalistic representations that would capture differences between the root and past-tense forms of both regular and irregular English verbs while allowing for the emergence of any possible generalizations between present- and past-tense forms, both the input and output banks of the network were designed to "comprehend" and "produce" individual letters of infinitives and past-tense forms as clusters of phonological features and word-boundary information.

The network was trained by presenting it with infinitival forms (in the form of sequences of letters, which were themselves represented by phonological features) together with a random activation of the output nodes and the infinitives' correct past-tense forms (representing a "teacher" function, the idea being that children receive only correct input from the environment).[3] Using a learning algorithm, the network gradually adjusted its input-output connection weights such that there was a high probability that its output would eventually match the desired output pattern.

The training period was designed to emulate Rumelhart and McClelland's (1986) characterization of the input that a child would be exposed to during the time he or she was acquiring English. According to them, a child will first learn about the present and past tenses of the most frequently occurring verbs. This was represented by first training their network for ten epochs, or cycles, on the ten most frequently occurring English verbs of their training set. Following this, their network was trained for 190 cycles on an additional 410 medium-frequency verbs. During this time, the network progressed in its learning such that by the end of its training, it had all but mastered the infinitive-to-past-tense mappings for the 420 verbs. Close examination of the progression of learning revealed some surprising results, among which were the following:

- Similar to what has been noted to occur during child acquisition of English, the network exhibited "u-shaped" learning behavior with respect to irregular verbs. While the network coped equally well with regulars and irregulars for the first ten verbs, performance with irregulars initially dropped upon the introduction of the 410 medium-frequency verbs such that the network incorrectly overgeneralized the regular -ed ending to the infinitival forms of irregulars, including both new irregulars and those that had been among the first ten verbs (i.e., irregulars that the network had previously gotten right). The network needed an additional thirty cycles of training before it began to gradually retreat from its overgeneralizations. By the time the two-hundred-cycle training phase had been completed, the network performed almost flawlessly with both regulars and irregulars, though it continued to perform somewhat better with regulars than with irregulars.

- Across nine different morphological classes of irregular verbs and three classes of regular verbs,
  the network showed overall error patterns similar
  to those made by preschool children in a child
  language-acquisition study (Bybee and Slobin,
  1982). The resemblance between preschool-child
  and network performance was particularly striking with verbs that are the same for the present
  and past tenses (e.g., *beat, fit,* etc.), but it was also
  observable with irregulars having stem-vowel
  changes (e.g., *deal, hear,* etc.).
- In terms of the pattern of occurrence for the two
  types of regularizations of irregular verbs that
  have been observed in the child language-acquisition literature (infinitive + *-ed,* for instance,
  eated, and past tense form + *-ed,* for instance,
  ated; Kuczaj, 1977), the network performed similarly to child language-learners, although this was
  true of only a subset of the verbs that the network
  was trained upon. Much as older children produce increasing proportions of forms such as
  ated relative to forms such as *eated,* over time the
  network also produced an increasing proportion
  of incorrect forms such as *ated.*
- With respect to the eighty-six low-frequency verbs
  (seventy-two regular, fourteen irregular) that
  were not a part of the network's original training
  set, Rumelhart and McClelland (1986) found that
  the network coped quite well with these novel
  items: 84 percent of the correct past-tense features were chosen with the novel irregulars, and
  92 percent of the correct past-tense features were

chosen with the novel regulars. What is more, when the network was allowed to make unconstrained responses (that is, when the network was allowed to generate its own past-tense forms rather than select one possible past-tense form from among several provided to it), it very often freely generated correct irregular and regular past-tense forms.

Rumelhart and McClelland's (1986) network had accomplished all of its learning strictly on the basis of allowing its connection weights to be tuned by the statistical regularities present in its input (here, the 420 regular and irregular English verbs it had been trained upon). Crucially, the network did not rely upon rules to learn regular past-tense forms for novel verbs or to learn semiregularities among the irregulars (e.g., *sing-sang, ring-rang,* etc.). This is because in connectionist accounts of language processing (and in connectionist accounts of human cognition in general), instances of rulelike behavior may be observed, but these instances cannot be attributed to the application of rules because there are no rules anywhere in a connectionist system. Thus, in a system where all knowledge, linguistic or otherwise, is reducible to the sum total of inhibitory and excitatory connections between and within layers of nodes in a network, the notion of "rule" is viewed as nothing more than a convenient fiction devoid of ecological validity; while it may be possible to state a rule that adequately captures a widespread generalization such as "to form the English regular past tense, add *-ed* to the end of a regular verb's infinitival form," rules play no role in how the connectionist network actually learns that generalization. In other words, a rule may describe what the network knows, but it does not describe how the network learns what it knows. Instead, learning occurs strictly through a probabilistic, data-driven (i.e., bottom-up) process.

An Answer to the Connectionist Challenge: Pinker and Prince, 1988

The results of Rumelhart and McClelland's (1986) study were highly provocative in that they called into question the classical (i.e., symbolic) approaches to the learning and mental representation of language. Symbolically oriented researchers were quick to respond to the connectionists' claims. In fact, an entire special issue of the journal *Cognition* was devoted to a critical examination of connectionism (volume 28, 1988). In that special issue, Steven Pinker and Alan Prince (Pinker and Prince, 1988) published a critique of Rumelhart and McClelland's study in which nearly a dozen objections were raised, pertaining to virtually all of the findings obtained with the neural network. For the sake of brevity, and to focus on the main shortcomings of the model, I will discuss here only Pinker and Prince's objections to the four main findings of Rumelhart and McClelland outlined above. With respect to the first of these findings, Pinker and Prince argued that in contrast to the input characteristics of the data that the Rumelhart and McClelland network was trained upon, parental speech to children does not change in its proportion of regular to irregular verbs over time, as longitudinal studies such as Brown (1973) indicate. Thus, there is a mismatch between observed input patterns to human children and the patterns in the input with which Rumelhart and McClelland trained their network. Pinker and Prince further reasoned that if children do not receive input pertaining to regular and irregular past tenses in the proportions that the neural network did yet still go through a period of overgeneralization before gradually sorting out the regular and irregular past tenses, then children's overgeneralizations and u-shaped development must be due to factors other than environmental ones. Put differently, the network was able to model a period of overgeneralizations and u-shaped development, but it did so on the basis of input patterns that no human child is likely to be exposed to.

Concerning the second point above, that the network error patterns of nonchanging verbs such as *hit* were similar to error patterns observed with human children, Pinker and Prince argued that there are several equally plausible accounts (two of which are actually rule-based) for the network's early acquisition and overgeneralization of these verbs. They further argued that the results may be attributable not to the network's design per se, but to an unintended consequence of the phonological features used to represent infinitives and past-tense forms within the network. In the absence of evidence from studies of children's acquisition of groups of words that do not embody a confound between a common phonological property and the phonological shape of a suffix (for example, the group of nonchanging English verbs ending in *t* and *d*, when *t* and *d* are also regular past-tense allomorphs), Pinker and Prince argued that it is impossible to tease apart an input-based account from a rule-based account of how children learn to cope with this class of verbs. For these reasons, Pinker and Prince held that the network's being able to model the acquisitional data is itself not sufficient to demonstrate the superiority of the network over other possible accounts.

Concerning the third point made above, that the network performed similarly to child language learners by producing an increasing number of incorrect irregular past-tense forms such as *ated* relative to forms such as *eated,* Pinker and Prince noted that this output pattern was observed only during the trials when the network was given a choice of responses (i.e., not during testing with the eighty-six novel verbs). They further observed that if the same strength-of-activation criterion used for determining a likely response from the network during testing with the eighty-six novel low-frequency regular and irregular verbs had been applied to these irregulars, the network would not actually have activated many forms such as *ated.* Pinker and Prince also cite a more tightly controlled follow-up child study (Kuczaj, 1978) in which forms such as *ated* were, over time, observed to increase but then decrease relative to forms such as *eated.* By this measure, the error patterns of children and of the network do not match so closely. The one plausible hypothesis for the source of the network's behavior with these items was incorrect blending. That is, with infinitival forms such as *eat* the network applies both the irregular past-tense change, producing *ate,* and the regular past-tense change, producing *eated;* the double marking results from a blending of the two different past-tense forms. Following a close examination of the relevant child data, Pinker and Prince observed that incorrect blending does not appear to be an active process in children. Instead, Pinker and Prince argued that in children, such errors most likely result from correctly applying an inflectional rule to an incorrect base form (i.e., applying *-ed* to *ate* rather than to *eat*) and not from incorrectly blending *ate* and *eated.*

With respect to claims of how well the Rumelhart and McClelland network coped with novel verbs, Pinker and Prince observed that approximately a third of the seventy-two novel regular infinitives prompted some form of an incorrect response from the network. Oddly, in a very few cases the model failed to provide a response at all. Among actual responses that were incorrect, some involved stem vowel changes that had not been strongly represented in the training set (e.g., *shipt* from *shape*), some included double markings of the past tense (e.g., *typeded* from *type*), and some were simply difficult to classify (e.g., *squakt* from *squawk*). From these findings, Pinker and Prince concluded that the network had failed to learn many of the productive patterns represented in the 336 verbs (2 high frequency, 334 medium frequency) that it had been trained on. Moreover, Pinker and Prince suggested that the errors the network made were not reminiscent of errors that humans are likely to make.

Ultimately, Pinker and Prince concluded that the Rumelhart and McClelland PDP network fell short of offering a viable alternative to classical, symbol-based approaches to the learning and mental representation of the English past tense. Aside from the above-noted differences between human and network performance arguing against the network's viability as a model of human performance, Pinker and Prince also made a further, crucial observation: while the network was able to represent the phonological features of both regular and irregular infinitival and past-tense forms (through its use of distributed representations), by design it was unable to represent higher-order constructs (i.e., symbols) such as roots, infinitives, and past-tense forms. The inability of the network to represent these and other classes of linguistic objects meant that unlike humans, it was unable to form new words through well-attested processes of word formation such as reduplication (i.e., creating a new word by repeating the sound sequence of another word, for example, *bam-bam, boo-boo, can-can,* etc.). Consequently, since the model was limited to representing an infinitive not as a particular kind of linguistic object (i.e., as an untensed verb) but as an undifferentiated set of activated phonological features, this means that it was unable to provide the past tense of any novel verb for which the infinitival form does not share enough features with the infinitives the network was trained on. Children are in fact able to provide past tenses of novel verbs, however (see the discussion at the beginning of this chapter). Pinker and Prince also offered evidence that a prediction the model makes for human language—that if in fact all verbs (irregular and regular) are simply mappings of phonological features to past-tense meanings, there should be no homophony (i.e., same-sounding words that have different meanings) among irregular verbs or between regular and irregular verbs—is not borne out by the facts of English. To take two examples, there are in fact irregular verbs, such as *ring* and *wring*, that have homophonous infinitival forms but different meanings and different past-tense forms. Additionally, there are regular-irregular inflectional contrasts such as with the verb *hang*, which in the past tense can be either regular *hanged* (i.e., executed) or irregular *hung* (i.e., suspended). Such contrasts should not exist according to a straightforward mapping of features to past-tense meaning.

Other language items, such as words, roots, and affixes, that argue in favor of representations, and by extension in favor of symbolic representations, include verbs that have been derived from nouns or adjectives. For example, one of the senses of the verb *fly* takes an irregular past tense (i.e., *flew*); another, baseball-related sense of the verb *fly* takes a regular past tense with *-ed* (i.e., *flied*, as in *He flied out to center field*). How can it be that one past-tense form of this verb is irregular, while the other is regular? The explanation for these and other similar regular and irregular past-tense pairings is that the root form of one of these senses—the derived sense—is not an irregular verb but is instead a noun or an adjective. In the case of the derived sense of the verb *fly*, the root of the verb is most likely a noun, *fly ball*. Since its root is not an irregular verb, its past tense is not irregular, and thus its past tense is formed through adding the regular past-tense ending -*ed*. Through these and other examples, Pinker and Prince argued for the necessity of symbolic representations for words, roots, and affixes; comparisons of human performance and network capability suggest that distributed phonological features alone are not sufficient to give rise to the observable facts of the English past tense. The fact that the network would fail where people succeed points to a need to be able to represent words, roots, and affixes as abstract symbols.

In a subsequent set of observations in the same 1988 critique, Pinker and Prince systematically highlighted contrasts between regular and irregular past-tense verbs, with the goal of supporting their hypothesis that as a class, irregular verbs constitute a "partly structured list of exceptions" (p. 114). In contrast to regular verbs, classes of irregular verbs often bear phonological resemblance to one another (e.g., *blow, know, grow, throw; take, mistake, foresake, shake;* p. 115); often have a prototypical structure (e.g., all the *blow*-group verbs appear to have a prototypical phonological shape in that they tend to be consonant-liquid-diphthong sequences; p. 116); may have past-tense forms that are markedly less used, and therefore markedly more odd-sounding, than their present-tense forms (e.g., *bear-bore*), suggesting that for these verbs, the present- and past-tense forms have split in the minds of English speakers (p. 117); often have unpredictable membership, meaning that while a verb may have a strong phonological resemblance to a class of strong verbs, there is no way to predict from the verb's phonological shape whether it is in fact an irregular verb (e.g., *flow*, which resembles the verbs of the *blow* group but is regular; p. 118); and often exhibit morphological changes that appear to have no phonological motivation (e.g., the [ow] to [uw] present-past vowel change in the *blow* group is not conditioned by the vowel's surrounding phonemes; p. 119). Taken together these facts suggest that, again in contrast to regular verbs, the irregular verbs constitute a closed system, that is, aside from a very few exceptions, it remains a group of verbs to which no new members have been admitted in the recent history of the language. To explain the status of irregular and regular verbs in the minds of English speakers, Pinker and Prince (1988, p. 122) advanced the following proposal: in contrast to regular verbs, which are generated by a regular rule of past-tense formation and are thus not subject to factors related to human memory, the past-tense forms of irregular verbs are memorized, and as such are subject to memory-related factors—in particular, to variations in lexical frequency and to family resemblance.

Example of a Dual-Mechanism Theory: Words and Rules Theory

While not tested by Pinker and Prince (1988), words and rules theory would later be revisited and gradually elaborated upon by Pinker and his collaborators (see, e.g., Prasada and Pinker, 1993). In its most recent form (Pinker, 2000; Pinker and Ullman, 2002), words and rules theory holds that regular forms in English are the product of abstract, algebraic rules, while irregular forms in English are items that are stored in and retrieved from a partly associative lexical memory. Thus, in its division of language into words and rules, words and rules theory appeals to a traditional linguistic distinction between a repository of words (a mental lexicon) and a productive, rule-based combinatorial system (a grammar).

Words and rules theory contrasts with connectionism and other single-mechanism accounts of language processing in that it does not hold that all processing proceeds from pattern association. As we saw earlier, a network relying upon a simple association of phonological features and meaning would simply be unable to produce (and therefore be unable to account for) a number of existing irregular forms and regular-irregular past-tense contrasts in English. Again, as we saw earlier, what the pattern associator lacked was a way of representing higher-order constructs such as roots, verbs, nouns, and words—that is, symbolic representations. As Pinker and Prince (1988) argued, it is only through appealing to these and other symbolic representations that the language data they discussed can be accounted for.

However, words and rules theory also contrasts with traditional, rule-based accounts of the morphological structure of English (Chomsky and Halle, 1968). Such accounts attempt to characterize both regular and irregular inflection in terms of underlying, or base, forms and phonetic, or surface, forms with a series of ordered rules applying to underlying forms in order to produce the surface forms we actually utter. For example, according to Chomsky and Halle (1968), the regular past-tense suffix -ed has an underlying form of /d/; depending upon the final consonant of the verb it is attached to, either a devoicing rule (that is, a rule that changes a segment from voiced to unvoiced) or a vowel epenthesis rule (that is, a rule that inserts a schwa between the final consonant of the root and the past-tense suffix when the two share common phonological features, specifically, place and manner of articulation) may apply to produce the appropriate surface form from the underlying regular past-tense form /d/. With a verb that ends in a voiced consonant, such as *beg*, neither rule applies, and the regular past tense is *begged*, pronounced [bɛgd]. With a verb ending in a voiceless consonant, such as *bake*, the devoicing rule will apply, producing the surface form *baked*, pronounced [beikt]. With verbs ending in a consonant that matches /d/ in terms of its place and manner of articulation, such as *fade*, the rule of vowel epenthesis applies, producing the surface form *faded*, pronounced [feidɪd]. Phonological rules such as these can accurately predict the form of any regular English verb. However, as mentioned earlier in the discussion of Pinker and Prince (1988), many of the present-past sound changes among the irregular verbs do not appear to have phonological motivation, i.e., they are not phonologically conditioned the way they are for the regular past-tense forms. Additionally, as observed by Pinker (2000), Chomsky and Halle's determination to capture all of the semiregularities with a very few rules ultimately led to their having to posit some underlying forms that, while plausible in the sense that they often reflected documented sound changes in the historical development of English, were almost unbelievable as viable representations in the minds of living speakers of English. To take one example, according to Chomsky and Halle the underlying form of the English verb *fight* [fait] is /fiçt/, in which the /ç/ represents a sound similar to the Germanic-sounding *ch* in *Bach*. Furthermore, adhering to rules at all cost sometimes meant having to make rather surprising claims concerning irregulars—for instance, that an irregular verb such as *keep* is in fact regular, in the sense that its past-tense form is fully derivable through vowel shifting, vowel laxing, and devoicing rules.

    Words and rules theory holds that irregulars are neither the product of traditional phonological rules, nor the product of an unstructured associative memory. Instead, irregulars are said to be organized in memory in a fashion somewhat reminiscent of semiproductive "lexical redundancy rules" (see, e.g., Aronoff, 1976; Jackendoff, 1975). Such rules do not build structure but instead impose constraints upon the range of possible structures specified by the structure-building rules. Recall that families of irregular verbs appear to have a prototypical phonological shape, yet they often have unpredictable membership and tend moreover to exhibit morphological changes that appear to have no phonological motivation. Pinker and his colleagues hold that these facts reflect the organization of irregulars in a partially associative memory that captures certain similarities among the irregulars. This organization serves to enhance a speaker's recall of members of the irregular verb family; it also allows limited generalizations, by analogy, to novel forms from existing irregular forms. In contrast to irregulars, regular items tend to be the product of symbolic rules. In the case of the regular past tense, a rule-based (i.e., grammatical) process combines the past-tense suffix *-ed* with the root form of any regular verb to produce a regular past-tense verb. During actual language processing, these two systems are said to work in parallel. If a search of the partly associative memory turns up a stored form, then a signal from the associative-memory system inhibits the grammatical system from computing a regular past tense. If the memory-system search fails to turn up a lexical entry, however, then the grammatical system computes the regular past tense.

There are a number of empirical implications for the words-and-rules-theory-based claims made above. In the context of behavioral studies, which is the main focus of this book, these include the following:

1. To the degree that it is a symbolic, combinatorial process and not the product of a partly associative

memory, regular inflection should pattern with acknowledged indices of symbolic processing.

2. To the degree that it is the product of a partly associative memory and not the product of symbolic processing, irregular inflection should pattern with acknowledged indices of associative memory.

Differently stated, regular and irregular inflection should be psychologically distinguishable.

Pinker (2000), Ullman (2001a), and Pinker and Ullman (2002) all offer evidence not only of the psychological separability of regular and irregular English inflectional processes, but also of their distributional and neurological separability. In the present work, I will be focusing on the applicability of words and rules theory to the online processing of French. As a backdrop to the experiments that I report in chapters 3–6, I will first introduce the notion of *priming* in the context of online studies. Following this, I present several English language behavioral studies that in addition to the work of Pinker and colleagues discussed above, have often been cited in support of words and rules theory.

II

Priming and Priming Studies

Much of the behavioral evidence cited in support of words and rules theory has come from studies in which people perform language-related tasks under tightly controlled (i.e., experimental) conditions. One such task is deciding whether a string of visually presented letters is a word. When the string of letters is preceded by other information, the decision task is said to be "primed." Because priming studies figure prominently as supporting evidence for words and rules theory, I will begin this chapter with a review of the notion of priming, with special emphasis on the rationale behind the variants of the primed lexical-decision task that will later be featured in my own experiments.

In a classic study, Meyer and Schvaneveldt (1971) demonstrated that subjects in a lexical-decision experiment were faster to respond affirmatively to a word such as *doctor* when that word was preceded by a semantically related word, for example, *nurse,* than when it was preceded by an unrelated word, for example, *sandal.* This facilitatory effect of a "prime" (in this case, the word *nurse*) on a stimulus or target (here, the word *doctor*) is said to reflect a change in the subject's cognitive system that results in a reduction in the time needed to react to a target compared to a baseline condition (i.e., the prior presentation of an unrelated word, in this case the word *sandal*). In early spreading-activation accounts of the semantic priming effect (e.g., Anderson, 1983; Collins and Loftus, 1975; Neely, 1977), the presentation of the prime was thought to activate all other lexical entries that were semantically related to it, thereby activating the target before it was actually presented in the experiment. Researchers theorized that this activation of the target through prior presentation of a related prime was what led to reduced response latencies to the target (for an alternative compound-cue view of semantic priming, see McKoon and Ratcliff, 1992; Ratcliff and McKoon, 1988; 1994).

The facilitatory effect of priming in various linguistic domains (e.g., semantic, phonological, morphological, orthographic, and syntactic) has generated much discussion concerning the locus of the facilitatory effect (Feustel, Shiffrin, and Salasoo, 1983; Forster, 1999; Forster and Davis, 1984; Jacoby, 1983). Particularly in cases where there is substantial phonological, morphological, or orthographic overlap between primes and targets (e.g., *wail-whale, whale-whales, whael-whale*), and especially in the case of repetition priming (i.e., when an item is used to prime itself), researchers have sought to establish whether priming effects in fact reflect the facilitation of automatic stimulus processing, as originally proposed. Instead, as some researchers have suggested, priming effects may reflect the facilitated operations of a central-executive or supervisory system (for discussions of such systems, see Fodor, 1983; Shallice, 1988) in that the memory trace of a prime merely facilitates a task-dependent decision to respond. According to this standpoint, priming effects may not have a lexical basis at all (a rather disquieting possibility).

In classic repetition, or long-term, priming experiments, the subject is first asked to study a list of words. This study period is then followed by a test period in which the subject makes lexical decisions on the items reviewed during the study period together with novel items, a subset of which are related in a crucial way to words presented in the study phase. Given the near impossibility of controlling for item resemblance at every level except the one of interest, researchers have sought to develop variations of the priming technique that would be resistant to the criticism that priming reflected episodic or strategic (i.e., related to the study period or, more generally, to the context of the experiment) rather than lexical factors. One such technique, *masked priming,* has received much attention as it appears to offer researchers a considerable measure of security against episodic or strategic effects within visual lexical-decision experiments (Forster and Davis, 1984; see also Forster, 1998; Grainger and Segui, 1990; Rajaram and Neely, 1992; Sereno, 1991). The design of a masked-priming study is similar in most respects to that of a classic-priming study, with one crucial difference: while subjects are aware of the study period in a classic-priming experiment, they are for all intents and purposes unaware of it in a masked-priming experiment. This is because in masked-priming experiments, primes are displayed for extremely short durations, roughly within the range of thirty-five to sixty milliseconds. By using both forward and backward masking, that is, by preceding the prime with a string of unrelated symbols or letters and by having the target immediately follow, primes displayed for between roughly thirty-five and sixty milliseconds are for most people effectively subliminal. The chief advantage of this technique is that if a subject is not consciously aware of having seen a prime, then it is unlikely that the prime could influence the subject's conscious decision to respond. It is for this reason that in contrast to long-term priming effects, masked-priming effects are thought to be largely free of episodic or strategic influences and to reflect unconscious, automatic lexical processing.

Forster and Davis (1984) were among the first to pioneer the masked repetition-priming technique (for the first modern uses of this technique, see Marcel, 1980; 1983). In their study, they identified three different kinds of behavioral dissociations between long-term priming and masked priming. First, they noted that masked-priming effects were obtained with words, but not with nonwords. Since only words will actually have lexical entries, this finding suggested that masked priming reflects lexical processes. Second, Forster and Davis observed that low- and high-frequency targets yielded similar priming effects when preceded by masked primes, but that low-frequency targets yielded stronger priming effects than high-frequency targets in long-term priming. Forster and Davis held that for both masked and long-term priming, primes open their lexical entries, and that in both cases, the entry is still open when the target is presented. They also assumed that the time needed to open a lexical entry is independent of a lexical item's frequency. If masked priming reflects lexical rather than episodic processes, it would be expected for the technique to yield similar priming for both high- and low-frequency targets. Finally, Forster and Davis observed that masked-priming effects are extremely short-lived, whereas long-term priming effects are not. Taken together, the findings and conclusions of Forster and Davis suggest that masked priming is superior to long-term priming for exploring the time course of lexical processing without episodic or strategic influences.

Owing to the wide variety of timing- and stimulus-related variables used in masked-priming studies, it is difficult to make categorical statements concerning the task's ability to measure processing in a given linguistic domain. However, with respect to the study of morphological relationships on lexical processing, research has shown that with masked priming, one can observe morphological priming independently of semantic or orthographic priming (for representative studies, see Frost, Forster, and Deutsch, 1997; Grainger, Colé, and Segui, 1991).

In another priming technique, cross-modal priming, primes are presented in one modality (e.g., auditorily), while targets are presented in another (e.g., visually). The motivation for crossing modalities is to encourage subjects to rely upon amodal mental representations, that is, upon mental representations of the prime and stimulus that are independent of the modality through which they were transmitted during the experiment.

Word-Level Priming Studies with English

Studies have successfully used various forms of priming to address a wide variety of processing phenomena, including the morphological processing of isolated words in the context of testing theories of lexical representation such as words and rules theory. In morphological priming, as the name implies, the primes are inflected or derived words, and the base or root forms serve as targets, or vice versa. Studies of morphological priming have demonstrated that under varying prime-target presentation conditions (e.g., with masked primes, cross-modal primes, etc.), inflected or derived word forms will prime their root forms (see Drews, 1996, for a recent review of findings with this paradigm). For instance, Stanners et al. (1979) used a variant of long-term morphological priming to investigate the processing of regular and irregular English verbs and their nominal and adjectival derivatives. They found that while irregularly inflected items did not prime their stems, regularly inflected items and their derivatives did. Napps (1989) used long-term priming to examine the morphological processing of nouns and their regularly inflected forms (e.g., *car-cars*) and of nouns and other orthographically but not morphologically related nouns (e.g., *car-card*). Napps found that while regularly inflected plurals primed their base forms, no priming was observed between orthographically similar but morphologically unrelated items. Marslen-Wilson, Hare, and Older (1995) reported on studies that used cross-modal morphological priming to examine the processing of the English past tense in regular and irregular verbs. These studies essentially confirmed the findings of Stanners et al. (1979), namely, that while regularly inflected English past tenses prime their stems, irregularly inflected ones do not (for similar findings and conclusions, see also Fowler, Napps, and Feldman, 1985, and Marslen-Wilson, Hare, and Older, 1993). By and large, the results and conclusions of these morphological-priming studies have been interpreted as evidence in favor of dual-mechanism morphological-processing models in which regularly inflected items are the product of symbolic rules that assemble them on the fly, while irregulars are recalled from an associative memory (cf. Pinker and Prince, 1991; Pinker, 2000).

Word-Level Priming Studies with Other Languages

As pointed out by Orsolini and Marslen-Wilson (1997) and by Marslen-Wilson and Tyler (1998), in order to rule out the possibility that the behavioral dissociation observed between regulars and irregulars is an idiosyncratic feature of English and therefore not reflective of universal facts of language processing, it is imperative to investigate languages other than English that offer similar contrasts of regular and irregular items. Studies have in fact been conducted with languages including German, Italian, and French, with mixed results. For instance, Clahsen and his colleagues have conducted studies using various forms of priming to investigate the morphological processing of German regular -s plurals such as *Waggon-Waggons,* "wagon-wagons"; irregular -er plurals such as *Kind-Kinder,* "child-children"; regular -t past participles such as *kaufen-gekauft,* "buy-bought"; and irregular -n past participles such as *lügen-gelogen,* "lie-lied" (see, e.g., Clahsen, 1999; Clahsen, Eisenbeiss, and Sonnenstuhl-Henning, 1997; Marcus et al., 1995; Sonnenstuhl, Eisenbeiss, and Clahsen, 1999;). By and large, the results from the German studies have been interpreted as supporting a dual-mechanism model of morphological processing.

In contrast, studies conducted with Romance languages have not yielded results consistent with the dual-mechanism hypothesis. Using cross-modal priming and elicitation of inflected forms, Orsolini and Marslen-Wilson (1997) examined the morphological processing of Italian past definite and past participle forms. Recognizing the obvious differences between English and Italian (i.e., English is morphologically poor while Italian is morphologically rich, and in its irregular verb conjugations, Italian has a high degree of regularity and phonological predictability relative to English), the authors present linguistic, acquisitional, and distributional evidence in support of their contention that Italian past definites and past participles show clear patterns of regularity and irregularity that should prompt the same regular-irregular behavioral dissociation observed with English. Orsolini and Marslen-Wilson found significant priming with both regular and irregular forms of past definites and past participles. The written elicitation data, obtained from having subjects produce past tenses of novel verb forms within sentential contexts, also failed to reveal a pattern interpretable within the dual-mechanism model. Noting that the regular versus irregular English past-tense distinction may represent a cross-linguistically extreme morphological contrast, Orsolini and Marslen-Wilson concluded that the dual-mechanism account might be too closely tied to the peculiarities of English to serve as an underpinning for a universal model of morphology.

Through two priming experiments (one masked and one cross-modal), Meunier and Marslen-Wilson (2000; see also Meunier and Marslen-Wilson, 2004) examined the processing of regular and irregular present-tense French verbs. Like Italian, French exhibits a great deal of predictability, even among its irregular verbs. On the basis of conjugation patterns, Meunier and Marslen-Wilson identified and tested regular verbs ending in -er (e.g., *manger*, "to eat") and three other classes of verbs: regular verbs also ending in -er but containing spelling changes in their paradigms (e.g., *semer*, "to sow"), irregular -re verbs containing spelling changes in their paradigms (e.g., *peindre*, "to paint"), and idiosyncratic irregulars with suppletive forms in their paradigms (e.g., *aller*, "to go").[4] Equivalent amounts of priming with both regulars and irregulars were observed in both experiments. Meunier and Marslen-Wilson concluded that their findings were inconsistent with the dual-mechanism model.

Cross-Modal Sentence-Level Priming Studies with English

The design of some priming techniques allows for the researcher to explore processing questions beyond the word

level. To take one example, cross-modal priming has been successfully adapted to research that explores sentence processing. For instance, Nicol and Swinney (1989) reported a series of
experiments by Swinney et al. (1988) that investigated the
phenomenon of *wh*-movement in English. Briefly, in *wh*-
movement, expressions beginning with words that start with
wh- (for instance, *which, what, who,* etc.) are preposed, that is,
they appear before their canonical sentential positions. According to some theories of syntax (e.g., Chomsky, 1981; 1995),
this movement results in a trace of the expression being left at
its original, underlying location. The experiments by Swinney
et al. (1988) were designed to see whether English speakers were
sensitive to the relationship between moved expressions and
their traces. Subjects listened to sentences in which an expression did not appear in its canonical position, for example, *A
squirrel ate the flowers which you worked so hard to plant in the
garden last fall,* in which *flowers* precedes rather than follows
the verb *plant* (cf. *You worked so hard to plant the flowers in the
garden last fall*). At three different moments while the sentence
was playing out (the pre-trace, trace, and post-trace points, as
depicted in sentence 2.1 below), visual probes in the form of
written words appeared on a computer screen:

> 2.1 A squirrel ate the flowers which the gardener
> worked so hard [pre-trace point] to plant [trace
> point] in the yard [post-trace point] last fall.

The subject's task was to make lexical decisions on the visually presented words, which in these studies were semantically related to *flowers* (e.g., *roses*). Consistent with the notion
that *wh*-moved expressions are reactivated at their trace points,
faster reaction times (RTs) to lexical decisions were recorded at

the trace and post-trace points than at the pre-trace point. In a control condition, subjects made lexical decisions on visually presented words that were semantically related to *gardener* and that appeared at the same pre-trace, trace, and post-trace points. Here, Swinney and colleagues observed faster RTs to lexical decisions at the pre-trace point, but not at the trace point and post-trace point. The results of these studies and others (see Nicol, Fodor, and Swinney, 1994) have suggested that in English, *wh*-traces prime their antecedents.

Selected Word-Level English-Language Behavioral Studies Supporting Words and Rules Theory

A number of priming studies, including (in chronological order) Stanners et al., 1979, Kempley and Morton, 1982, and Napps, 1989, have been cited as supporting words and rules theory (see Pinker, 2000). Interestingly, none of these studies sought to investigate words and rules theory directly; indeed, they all predate the creation of the theory. Yet for each study, the findings of regular-irregular processing differences are readily accounted for by words and rules theory.

STANNERS ET AL., 1979

The study by Stanners and colleagues investigated the online storage and retrieval of morphologically complex English words. Specifically, their study used a lexical-decision task, in the context of repetition priming in the visual modality, to determine whether inflected verbs (including forms with third-person -*s*, regular past-tense -*ed*, and gerundive -*ing* and irregular past-tense forms) and nouns and adjectives derived from verbs had memory representations that were separate from their root forms. Stanners et al. conducted four experiments. Primes and targets were separated by a lag of six to fifteen items, and with a three-second inter-trial interval this amounted to a lag of fifteen to forty-five seconds between prime and stimulus presentation. All experiments had an equal number of real-word and nonword trials. Furthermore, all experiments were designed such that the time needed to make lexical decisions on all root forms of verbs (which were always the target form) could be compared under different conditions: when the root occurred by itself (i.e., as a prime), when the root had been primed by itself, or when it had been primed by one of its inflected or derived forms.

In experiment 1, twenty-four undergraduates made primed lexical decisions on sixty English verbs bearing third-person -s, regular past-tense -ed, and gerundive -ing inflections. Analyses indicated a main effect of repetition priming with the root forms of verbs; lexical decisions to root forms that had been primed by prior presentation of the root form were faster than the initial, or unprimed, presentation of that root form. Thus, given two presentations of *eat* separated by six to fifteen intervening words, subjects were faster to say that *eat* was a word the second time they saw it. A further finding from experiment 1 was that priming with the inflected forms was as effective as priming with the root forms. Statistically speaking, lexical decisions to root forms that had been primed by prior presentation of the corresponding inflected form were just as fast as lexical decisions to root forms that had been primed by the root forms themselves. Thus, given *eats* and *eat* in that order and separated by six to fifteen intervening words, subjects said that *eat* was a word just as fast as when *eat* had preceded *eat*.

In experiment 2, twenty undergraduates made primed lexical decisions on forty irregular past-tense English verbs.

Half of the verbs formed their past tense through changing one letter (e.g., *bent* vs. *bend*), while the other half of the verbs changed more than one letter to form their past tense (e.g., *sweep* vs. *swept*). Similar to experiment 1, experiment 2 was designed such that the time needed to make lexical decisions on the root forms of verbs (which as before were always the target form) could be compared under two conditions: when the root form had been primed by itself, or when it had been primed by its irregular past-tense form. Analyses indicated that as in experiment 1, and for both one-letter-change and more-than-one-letter-change past-tense forms, there was a main effect of repetition priming between root forms. However, in contrast to the previous experiment, it was not the case that priming with the inflected forms was as effective as priming with the root forms. Thus *bend* was a better prime for *bend* than was *bent*. A further analysis revealed that while root forms of irregular verbs were better primes for target root forms than were irregular past forms, there was still an observable priming effect of the irregular past-tense forms on root forms. That is, subjects were significantly faster to say that *bend* was a word when it had been preceded by *bent* than when *bend* had been preceded by some other word or nonword. Finally, a comparison between lexical-decision times for root and irregular past forms as primes revealed that decision times were longer with irregular past forms than with root forms.

In experiment 3, twenty undergraduates made primed lexical decisions on forty adjectives that had been derived from verbs. Half of the adjectives were derived through suffixation only, that is, with no spelling change in the root verb (e.g. *select-selective*) or, for a subset of these items, with a minimal spelling change (specifically, the dropping of a final -*e*). The derivation of the other half of the adjectives was more involved, generally involving a spelling change inside the root verb (e.g., *persuade-*

persuasive). The same derivational suffixes (-*ive*, -*ent*, -*ant*, and -*able*) were used with all forty adjectives. As in experiments 1 and 2, analyses again revealed a main effect of repetition priming between root verb forms. Similar to the finding of experiment 2, further analysis revealed that while root forms of verbs were better primes for target root forms than were derived adjectives, there was still a measurable priming effect of derived adjectives on root forms of verbs.

In experiment 4, twenty undergraduates again made primed lexical decisions, this time on forty nouns that had been derived from verbs (e.g., *appear-appearance*). As in experiment 3, half of the nouns were derived through a minimal spelling change (that is, either through no change to the root verb's spelling or, for a fraction of these items, through the dropping of a final -*e*). Derivational suffixes for these twenty nouns included -*ance*, -*ence*, -*tion*, and -*ion*. As before, the derivation of the other half of the nouns was more involved, generally entailing a spelling change inside the root verb (e.g., *receive-reception*). Derivational suffixes for these twenty nouns included -*tion* and -*ion*. Analyses revealed a main effect of repetition priming between root verb forms. As in experiments 2 and 3, root forms of verbs were better primes for target root forms than were derived nouns, but there was still a measurable priming effect of derived nouns on root forms of verbs.

Stanners's team concluded that the overall pattern of results—namely, measurable priming of root forms of verbs from both inflected and identical (i.e., root verb) forms, but weaker priming of root verb forms from adjectives and nouns derived from the root verb—did not support a purely semantically based account of the storage and retrieval of the items tested. They further concluded that a purely orthographically based account would also be suspect, since effects of orthography (i.e., minimal vs. more than minimal spelling change in experiments 2–4) were never observed. Instead, Stanners et al. proposed that their results were compatible with a view in which inflections and other highly regular orthographic processes facilitate the recovery of root forms during processing (i.e., the "rules" of words and rules theory). By contrast, due to their less-regular formation, irregular past tenses and derived nouns and adjectives may require language learners to create separate memory representations of those forms (i.e., the "words" of words and rules theory).

KEMPLEY AND MORTON, 1982

This is another study the findings of which are readily accommodated by words and rules theory (though again, this study predated words and rules theory). The point of departure for the article was the finding by Murrell and Morton (1974) that in the visual modality, morphologically related words (e.g., *seen* and *sees*) appear to prime one another almost as well as do identical words. Kempley and Morton wished to rule out the possibility that semantics played a facilitatory role in the long-lag (ten to forty-five minutes) priming observed by Murrell and Morton, and also to see whether the previously observed priming effects would emerge in the auditory modality.

In order to address these questions, Kempley and Morton observed how well listeners could recognize spoken words that had been partially masked with white noise (that is, with sound containing frequency components of equal amplitude over the entire spectrum). The researchers compiled a list of sixty morphologically related regular and irregular pairs of English words (e.g., *low-lowest* and *better-good*, respectively). One member of each regular or irregular pair was designated the test word, the other a related word. For each pair of words, Kempley and Morton added an orthographically similar but

semantically and morphologically unrelated word. The resulting regular- and irregular-based triads consisted of adjectives
(e.g., *low, lowest, local* and *better, good, letter*), nouns (e.g.,
party, parties, part and *thief, thieves, grief*), and verbs (e.g., *talk,
talked, cork* and *binds, bound, kinds*). The sixty triads of words
were recorded under two conditions: either partially masked
by white noise, or in the clear.

In the pre-test phase of the experiment, subjects ($n = 32$)
listened to the words that had been recorded in the clear and
rated them according to an imagery scale. The purpose of this
phase of the experiment was to prime the subjects for the test
phase of the experiment. During the test phase, subjects listened to and wrote down as best they could the words that had
been partially masked with white noise. Kempley and Morton
arranged all their words such that each word of a triad in the
test phase was preceded in the pre-test phase by a test word
(e.g., *low*), a morphologically related word (e.g., *lowest*), a similar word (e.g., *local*), or no word at all.

Subjects' scores during the test phase were tabulated according to two criteria: whether the subject reported having
heard the exact word or a word that was morphologically related to the test word. Kempley and Morton noted four main
results. First, with both regular and irregular words, subjects
were most accurate in noting words in the test phase when
the test word had been preceded by the same word in the pre-
test phase. Second, with regular words (but not with irregular
words), subjects were most accurate at recalling test words
such as *low* when they had been primed in the pre-test phase
with a morphologically related word such as *lowest*. Third,
with regular words (but again not with irregular words), subjects were as accurate at recalling morphologically related
words when they had been primed with morphologically re-

lated words as they were when they had been primed with test words (though subjects were more accurate at recalling test words when they had been preceded by test words than when they had been preceded by morphologically related words). Finally, subjects who heard similar words during the pre-test were no more accurate at recalling test words than were subjects who heard no word during the pre-test. From these findings, Kempley and Morton concluded that in the auditory domain, long-lag priming between regularly related words was morphemically (i.e., rule) based, while long-lag priming between irregularly related words was not (i.e., irregularly related items are presumably words in the words and rules theory sense). A further conclusion was that the priming effect observed between regular pairs was not semantically based, since semantic relationships presumably existed to the same degree in both regular and irregular pairs of test words.

NAPPS, 1989

Like the Stanners et al. (1979) and Kempley and Morton (1982) studies, this study also predated words and rules theory; nevertheless, its findings are again readily accommodated by it. Through three experiments, Napps set out to investigate whether a repetition-priming effect previously observed in the visual modality between morphemically related English words (Fowler, Napps, and Feldman, 1985) would manifest itself once strategic factors (i.e., factors related to how subjects cope with the experimental task), postaccess factors (i.e., factors related to checking of semantic relationships between prime and target), and episodic factors (i.e., factors related to the specific modality or context in which primes and targets occur) were controlled for.

In experiment 1 of Napps, seventy-two undergraduates made lexical decisions on forty-two English words. The first half of these words, which Napps termed "regular" words, were primed with either themselves or an inflected or a derived form of the original word (for example, the word *manage* was primed by *manage,* inflected form *manages,* and derived form *manager*). The second half of these words, which Napps called "sound-and-spelling change" words, were primed with either themselves or one of two suffixed forms of the original word, one in which suffixation was accompanied by a spelling change in the root form, and one in which suffixation was not accompanied by a root-form spelling change (for example, the word *assume* was primed by *assume, assumed,* and *assumption*). Napps attempted to attenuate any possible influence of episodic or strategic factors by greatly increasing the number of trials in which targets were filler words (i.e., words that were real but did not contain any morphological features of interest in the study), thereby reducing the proportion of prime-target sequences with discernible relationships. A further effort that Napps made to reduce episodic and strategic effects was to vary the lag, or number of noncritical words separating a critical prime-target pair; thus, in her study, prime-target pairs were separated by a lag of either zero, one, or ten noncritical words. Targets were always the root, or base, form of a word and were arranged such that lexical-decision times for all root forms could be compared under different conditions, that is, when the root occurred as a prime to a given target (i.e., an unprimed condition), when the root form had been primed by itself, and when it had been primed by one of its inflected or derived forms, or by one of its spelling-change or no-spelling-change forms.

Analysis of the reaction-time data for the regular words revealed that responses to identically, inflectionally, and derivationally primed targets were faster than to unprimed targets. Furthermore, reaction times to identically, inflectionally, and derivationally primed targets did not themselves differ statistically, nor was there an effect of lag. Essentially the same results were found with the prime-target pairs drawn from the sound-and-spelling-change words.

In experiment 2, Napps examined whether there would be repetition priming in the visual modality between root forms and their corresponding past-tense inflected forms. In this experiment, sixty-four undergraduates made primed visual lexical decisions on thirty English target words. Each target word had one of two possible primes, either an identical prime or a suppletive past-tense form of the target word. As in experiment 1, a high percentage of filler items was used to reduce any possible effects of episodic or strategic factors. Targets were always the root form of a word, and they were arranged such that lexical-decision times for all root forms could be compared under different conditions: when unprimed, when primed by themselves, or when primed by suppletive past-tense forms. Prime-target pairs were separated by a lag of zero, one, three, or ten noncritical words.

Analyses revealed that subjects responded faster to root forms that had been primed with both identical words and suppletive past-tense forms. Moreover, and in contrast to experiment 1, subjects responded faster to target words that had been primed by themselves than to targets that had been primed by suppletive past-tense forms. Finally, and again in contrast to experiment 1, there was an effect of lag such that at lags greater than one word, the priming effect of the suppletive forms disappeared (i.e., there was no statistical difference in reaction time between targets primed by suppletive forms and targets in the unprimed condition).

In experiment 3, Napps sought to rule out the possibility that the results of experiment 2 were due to semantic rather than morphological priming. In this final experiment, which, despite some differences in materials, was quite similar to experiments 1 and 2 in design and procedure, sixty undergraduates made lexical decisions on sixty-three English target words that had been primed in one of three ways: through identical priming (all sixty-three words), through an associated word (for a subset of thirty-two words), or through a synonym (for a subset of thirty-one words). For example, the target word *pain* was primed by itself and by *ache,* an associated word, while the target *mistake* was primed by itself and by *error,* a synonym.

An overall analysis revealed that subjects responded faster to associated primes and targets. Separate analyses of the associated and synonymous words in the unprimed and primed conditions indicated that associated words primed their targets, although they were less effective primes than were identical primes. By contrast, synonymous words did not prime their targets. Furthermore, the results of a survey indicated that the synonyms in experiment 3 had stronger semantic relationships between primes and targets than did the suppletive or associative words.

From her experiments, Napps concluded that while both regularly and irregularly inflected words are related to their root forms in the mental lexicon, the irregulars (i.e., words, in the words and rules theory sense) are less closely linked to their root forms than the regulars (i.e., rules). In fact, the pattern of results with irregulars was similar to the pattern observed with associated words.

Behavioral Studies Using Other Languages: Support for Words and Rules Theory?

Considered together, the studies described above offer converging evidence in favor of words and rules theory; however, studies examining lexical representation in other languages, particularly Italian and French, have not produced results that are readily accounted for with words and rules theory. Three such studies, one examining lexical representation in Italian, and the remaining two examining lexical representation in French, are presented below.

ITALIAN: ORSOLINI AND MARSLEN-WILSON, 1997

Orsolini and Marslen-Wilson investigated whether support for the dual-mechanism theory could be found using Italian past-tense forms. As the researchers noted, the available evidence for the theory had until that time been limited to studies using either English (e.g., Kim et al., 1991; Marslen-Wilson, Hare, and Older, 1995; Pinker, 1991; Prasada and Pinker, 1993) or German (e.g., Marcus et al., 1995). However, in order to be viable as a universal theory of lexical representation, the dual-mechanism theory needed to be tested with other languages. Orsolini and Marslen-Wilson created stimulus items from Italian because that language appeared to offer a regular-irregular opposition in verb inflectional morphology that was in many respects similar to the one found in English. To be more specific, Italian has a set of verbs that form the past definite and past participle with a highly predictable (i.e., regular) inflectional suffix and with no or minimal (and predictable) changes in the verb root, and it also has a set of verbs that form their past tenses through far less predictable means and with a greater degree and variety of change in the verb root.

There were two experiments. In experiment 1, twenty-four native speakers of Italian made lexical decisions on 144 Italian prime-target verb pairs. Forty-eight pairs contained regular verbs, forty-eight pairs contained irregular verbs, twenty-four pairs were homophonically (though not morphologically or semantically) related, and a final twenty-four pairs were semantically (though not morphologically or homophonically) related. For each of these prime-target pairs, primes were always in the past definite form, while targets were either infinitives or past participles. To establish a control condition, a second set of 144 word pairs was created in which each target was preceded not by its normal prime but by an unrelated control word that matched the prime in number of syllables and lexical frequency. The experiment was designed such that for a given target, half the subjects heard a normal prime, while the other half heard an unrelated control word. Items were presented cross-modally: primes were presented auditorily while targets were presented visually, immediately following the prime.

Results indicated that contrary to the predictions of the dual-mechanism theory, priming (in the form of faster lexical decisions to targets following test vs. control primes) was observed between both regular and irregular Italian prime-target pairs. Moreover, the priming effect with regular prime-target pairs did not differ in degree from the priming effect observed with irregular pairs. Comparisons between the homophonically and semantically related prime-target pairs and the control condition suggested that neither phonological resemblance nor similarity in meaning between prime and target contributed to the main findings. This surprising set of results suggested that unlike the English forms, both regular and irregular Italian past-tense forms may be rule based.

In experiment 2, Orsolini and Marslen-Wilson used an elicitation task. In this task, a subject is presented with a novel (i.e., nonce) item, whereupon he or she is supposed to produce (either through writing or speaking) a past-tense form of the novel item. As noted by Orsolini and Marslen-Wilson, previous studies with English (Bybee and Modor, 1983; Prasada and Pinker, 1993) have shown that subjects tend not to produce irregular past tenses in response to novel items unless the novel item bears a close phonological similarity to a real irregular. Put another way, if a novel item bears a phonological resemblance to an existing irregular verb, subjects tend to produce an irregular past tense in response to it; however, if a novel item bears little or no phonological resemblance to an existing irregular verb, subjects tend to produce a regular past-tense form. In their second experiment, Orsolini and Marslen-Wilson set out to see whether the regular-irregular behavioral opposition that had been observed with English would also be observed with regular and irregular Italian past-tense forms. The cross-modal priming results of experiment 1 suggested that both regular and irregular Italian past-tense forms were rule based. If this were true, then in an elicitation task there should be no effects of phonological resemblance for either Italian regulars or irregulars.

For experiment 2, Orsolini and Marslen-Wilson elicited the past-tense forms of 120 novel Italian untensed (i.e., infinitival) verbs from twenty native speakers of Italian. The novel verbs were either pseudoregular (i.e., resembling regular Italian verbs) or pseudoirregular (i.e., resembling irregular Italian verbs), and within each regularity condition, novel verbs bore either a high similarity, a root-only similarity, or a low similarity to existing Italian verbs (where similarity was defined according to the number of existing Italian verbs with which the nonce verbs rhymed). Elicitations were obtained through first providing a subject with a fictitious definition for the novel form, then asking the subject to use its past-tense form to fill in a blank in an otherwise complete Italian sentence.

Results indicated that unlike what had been observed in previous elicitation studies with English, there was no strong interaction between regularity and phonological similarity (i.e., degree of rhyming with existing verbs). Instead, and again rather surprisingly, Orsolini and Marslen-Wilson found that the regularity of elicited past-tense forms of both pseudoirregular and pseudoregular Italian verbs depended upon the similarity of the pseudo form to existing verbs. This result suggested that unlike regular past-tense inflection in English, and indeed in opposition to what had been found in experiment 1, regular past-tense inflection in Italian is not the product of a symbolic rule. Instead, the elicitation task of experiment 2 gave rise to effects suggesting that both regular and irregular past-tense inflections in Italian are listed in the lexicon. In reconciling the findings from Italian in experiments 1 and 2 with the results of existing studies using English, Orsolini and Marslen-Wilson proposed that the dual-mechanism theory be expanded: in addition to the default, rule-based type and the idiosyncratic, listed type of morphological representations appropriate for English, they suggested adding a third type of representation, which they termed *productive*. This latter type of representation, which is hypothesized to depend upon both productivity patterns and lexical information, would accommodate inflectional processes that "neither apply as a blind default to any member of an abstract category, nor require full listing of unanalyzable idiosyncratic procedures on a case by case basis" (Orsolini and Marslen-Wilson, 1997, p. 40).

FRENCH: ROYLE, JAREMA, AND KEHAYIA, 2002

Royle, Jarema, and Kehayia used simple (i.e., unprimed) and primed visual lexical-decision to investigate the effects of the frequency and morphological regularity of French verbs on both pathologically normal and developmentally language-impaired (DLI) francophone Canadians. Similar to Meunier and Marslen-Wilson, 2000, the Royle study varied the stem regularity of the verbs they tested. Royle and colleagues, however, also controlled for the relative frequency of their primes and targets, and they used purely phonological features as the basis for stem regularity, whereas Meunier and Marslen-Wilson had used conjugation classes. Thus while Royle, Jarema, and Kehayia defined their class of regulars the same way Meunier and Marslen-Wilson did, that is, as the class of -er verbs whose stems remain consistent with changes in person and number (e.g., *manger,* "to eat," *parler,* "to speak," etc.), their single class of irregulars comprised verbs whose stems have varying latent consonant surfacings and vowel changes according to variations in person and number inflections (e.g., *vendre,* "to sell," *tenir,* "to hold," *teindre,* "to dye," etc.). For example, the first person singular present indicative of *vendre* is *je vends* [ʒø vɑ̃], while the first person plural present indicative is *nous vendons* [nu vɑ̃ dɔ̃]. For *vendre* and other similar verbs, the change from singular to plural results in the surfacing of a latent stem consonant (in this case, [d]). Likewise, the first persons singular and plural of the present indicative of the verb *tenir* are *je tiens* [ʒø tjɛ̃] and *nous tenons* [nu tø nɔ̃], respectively. In this case, the singular-plural change prompts a glide-vowel alteration and a surfacing of a latent consonant in the stem of the verb (i.e., [j] changes to [ø], and [n] surfaces).

Based on their assumption that DLI francophone Canadians are morphologically "blind" and therefore not sensitive to the internal structure of polymorphemic words, the Royle team predicted that in contrast to their controls, who were expected to be sensitive to a verb's morphological structure and its frequency, their DLI subjects would be sensitive only to a word's frequency (in their study, verb frequency was operationalized as compound or cumulative frequency, rather than surface frequency). The DLI subjects' hypothesized response patterns were expected to be in proportion to a verb's decreasing frequency of occurrence: longer RTs and a greater number of errors were anticipated for items of lesser frequency. Furthermore, a verb's morphological structure was not predicted to be a factor in the DLI subjects' RTs or errors. Royle and colleagues hypothesized that for their controls, morphological structure would interact with frequency.

The results of both of their experiments supported their hypotheses. In the unprimed lexical-decision task, in analyses of both RTs and errors, controls demonstrated interactions between morphological structure and frequency: as words and rules theory would have predicted, responses to regular verbs were not dependent upon frequency (no surprise, as these would be seen as rule-based), while responses to frequent irregular verbs were both faster and more likely to be correct than were responses to infrequent irregular verbs (as would be expected if irregular verbs are stored in and retrieved from a partly associative memory). By contrast, DLI subjects in the unprimed lexical-decision task showed no such interactions;

instead, their responses revealed a sensitivity to a verb's frequency, but an insensitivity to a verb's regularity. Somewhat different results were obtained in the primed lexical-decision task. Here, controls showed no main effects of regularity for either prime or target, a trend toward an effect of target frequency, and no interactions. Surprisingly, the results of the primed lexical-decision task imply an across-the-board sensitivity to morphological structure for control subjects, in that primes activated the lexical entries of both regular and irregular targets, a result that is interpretable within words and rules theory, but only on the assumption that both regular and irregular French verbs are the product of rules.[5] While not showing a main effect of regularity, the DLI subjects did show a main effect of target frequency (with slower RTs to infrequent targets), as well as an interaction between prime and target frequency such that irrespective of a prime's frequency, infrequent targets always provoked longer RTs. Royle et al. concluded that in contrast to controls, DLI subjects were insensitive to the morphological structure of polymorphemic verbs and were instead sensitive only to an item's frequency.

FRENCH: MEUNIER AND MARSLEN-WILSON, 2000

Meunier and Marslen-Wilson examined whether the distinction between priming with regulars and no priming with irregulars, which had been observed with English and German, could be observed with French verbs. More specifically, using cross-modal and masked repetition-priming they addressed the question of whether a dual-mechanism or a single-mechanism account was the most appropriate to describe lexical representation in French. There were two experiments. In experiment

1, thirty-six French undergraduates made lexical decisions in a cross-modal repetition-priming study. Items were based upon twenty-four first-conjugation fully regular -er verbs (e.g., *parler*, "to speak"), twenty-four first-conjugation regular -er verbs with slight spelling changes (e.g., *semer*, "to sow"), twenty-four third-conjugation irregular -re verbs (e.g., *teindre*, "to dye"), and twenty-four highly irregular, suppletive verbs (e.g., *aller*, "to go"). Targets were always infinitival forms, while primes were either a regularly inflected form, an irregularly inflected form, or a control word matched for number of syllables, frequency, tense, and person with the regularly inflected form. The experiment was designed such that a given target was primed with a regularly inflected form for a third of the subjects, an irregularly inflected form for another third of the subjects, and a control word for the final third of the subjects. Table 2.1 below includes the mean RTs and degree of priming effect for the experiment.

Analyses indicated that subjects responded significantly faster to targets following regularly and irregularly inflected primes than they did to targets following control primes. Contrary to the expectations of the dual-mechanism theory, however, subjects did not show greater priming effects from regularly inflected primes than they did from irregularly inflected primes. That is, for this experiment, irregularly inflected verbs primed their targets as effectively as did regularly inflected primes.

In experiment 2, Meunier and Marslen-Wilson presented forty-two French undergraduates with the same prime-stimulus pairs as in experiment 1, but this time using masked priming (with prime durations of forty-seven milliseconds, effectively invisible to subjects). Two additional control conditions were used: one in which primes and targets were semantically related (e.g., *broyait*, "was grinding," and *mâcher*, "chew,"

Table 2.1. Mean RTs and degree of priming effect from experiment 1 of Meunier and Marslen-Wilson, 2000

Types of verbs	Primes	Targets	RT (ms.)	Priming effect (ms.)
Fully regular	aimerons	aimer	523	44
	aimons		530	37
	porterons			
	(control)		567	
Slight spelling changes	semons	semer	539	57
	sème		545	51
	votons			
	(control)		596	
Irregular	teindra	teindre	553	60
	teignent		551	62
	nichera			
	(control)		613	
Suppletive	allons	aller	544	49
	irons		545	48
	tenons			
	(control)		593	

respectively), and one in which primes and targets were orthographically related (e.g., *machine* and *mâcher,* respectively). Table 2.2 below includes the mean RTs and degree of priming effect for the experiment.

Overall findings using masked priming were very similar to the findings obtained using cross-modal priming: subjects again responded significantly faster to targets following regularly and irregularly inflected primes than they did to targets

Table 2.2. Mean RTs and degree of priming effect from experiment 2 of Meunier and Marslen-Wilson, 2000

Types of verbs	Primes	Targets	RT (ms.)	Priming effect (ms.)
Fully regular	aimerons	aimer	551	19
	aimons		552	18
	porterons			
	(control)		570	
Slight spelling changes	semons	semer	569	19
	sème		566	22
	votons			
	(control)		588	
Irregular	teindra	teindre	564	32
	teignent		578	18
	nichera			
	(control)		596	
Suppletive	allons	aller	560	32
	irons		578	14
	tenons			
	(control)		592	
Semantic and orthographic controls	broyait	macher	587	5
	machine		599	−7
	progrès			
	(control)		592	

following control primes. And once again, subjects failed to show greater priming effects from regularly inflected primes than from irregularly inflected primes. As the effects of both semantic and orthographic priming relative to control words were nonsignificant, it is very unlikely that the observed results were due to a simple form or meaning overlap between test primes and targets.

From the findings of experiments 1 and 2, Meunier and Marslen-Wilson concluded that the predictions of the dual-mechanism hypothesis—that lexical representation of regular forms is effectuated through a rule-based, symbolic processor, while representation of irregular forms proceeds through an associative memory system—were not borne out for French. As they noted, the finding that French irregular inflected verbs prime their infinitival forms as well as regular inflected verbs prime theirs is inconsistent with the notion that two different underlying processes are at work. Meunier and Marslen-Wilson considered but discarded as implausible the possibility that their results could be explained within a connectionist, single-mechanism account (e.g., MacWhinney and Leinbach, 1991; Plunkett and Marchman, 1993; Rumelhart and McClelland, 1986). Instead, they tentatively suggested two possible accounts of their findings in terms of the dual-mechanism model. In the first of these scenarios, a cross-linguistic difference in processing architecture is the source of the priming effects among stored irregular French verb forms. That is, English and French differ (according to this scenario) in terms of their general language-processing architecture. This difference in architecture is distinct from the presumed underlying difference in the way both English and French speakers store and retrieve irregulars but compute regulars; and it is this difference in general language-processing architecture that is captured in priming experiments with French verbs but not with English verbs. Though logically plausible, this account is somewhat speculative in that its empirical support stems from an interpretation of the priming effect as failing to reflect the type of processing (i.e., rule-based computation) it is standardly presumed to reflect in other, similar priming experiments.

More promising is their proposed account based upon French-English differences in morphological decomposability. In this view, French contrasts with English because English irregular verbs such as *went* are morphologically undecomposable (i.e., they are no longer seen as consisting of a stem form plus a suffix), while even the most irregular French verbs use the same suffixes as do regular French verbs. Relatedly, and again in contrast to English, variations in regularity with inflected French verbs are confined to the verb stems themselves. Taken together, these differences mean that regular suffixation applies in the case of both regular and irregular French verbs; this accounts for why Meunier and Marslen-Wilson observed priming with both regular and irregular tensed verbs. In terms of words and rules theory, this means that in contrast to English, all tensed French verbs are computed, that is, they are all the products of rules. More specifically, while English speakers may have to learn to selectively block the application of the default past-tense suffix when the past-tense form they need is a stored irregular (thereby preempting such forms as *breaked* or *comed*, according to words and rules theory), French speakers in every case are applying the same suffixes to both regular and irregular French verbs.

A further explanation offered by Meunier and Marslen-Wilson was based upon findings from English (Marslen-Wilson, Hare, and Older, 1995) and was also related to the notion of contrasting morphological decomposability for irregular French versus irregular English verbs. According to this explanation, in priming experiments with English, competition between possible stem forms of irregular verbs (the uninflected form of the irregular verb, for instance, *give,* and the verb's stored, irregular past-tense form, in this case, *gave*) may block lexical decomposition and subsequent regular suffixation, thereby preempting irregular-stem-plus-*ed* forms such as *gived.* With irregular verb forms in French, however, the process of competition would not result in blocking of decomposition and regular suffixation. This is because in contrast to English verbs, both regular and irregular forms of French verbs need to undergo morphological decomposition in order for their stem forms to be identified. As a result, there is no need to appeal to two distinct processes for regular and irregular forms of French verbs: according to this view, they are both the product of lexical decomposition and subsequent regular suffixation (i.e., of rules).

Conclusion

The findings of the studies just reviewed appear to challenge the efficacy of the dual-mechanism, or words-and-rules, model as the cornerstone of a universal theory of morphological processing. On the one hand, a considerable body of behavioral, neuropsychological, and developmental evidence suggests the existence of a word-rule dissociation in the representation and processing of English regular and irregular past tenses. On the other hand, a pattern of results interpretable within the dual-mechanism model has failed to materialize with languages other than English and German: in the Italian and French studies reviewed, equal amounts of priming were observed both for regular and irregular verb forms.

Is it possible that, as Orsolini and Marslen-Wilson (1997) suggested, the dual-mechanism model is simply too closely tied to the morphological patterns of English to have universal applicability? The findings from the Italian and French studies by Marslen-Wilson and colleagues certainly suggest that this might be so. We could argue, however, that claims of language specificity or calls for modification of the dual-mechanism model are premature. From a different perspective, the results of the French and Italian studies suggest only that behavioral dissociations do not exist between present or past-tense regular and irregular verbs. According to this view, since the results of the French and Italian studies do not rule out the existence of such dissociations in other kinds of morphological processes, they represent a call for alternatives to using Romance verbal inflectional morphology as a behavioral test bed for words and rules theory.

Meunier and Marslen-Wilson (2000) acknowledge the high degree of richness and regularity that characterizes French verbal morphology. They further note that English and French verbal morphology differ in terms of relative morphological decomposability. These observations seem to suggest a basic difference between regularity and irregularity in the French verbal system and regularity and irregularity in the English verbal system: in the case of French, both regular and irregular verbs are decomposable, while in English only the regular past tenses can be said to be decomposable. Thus, irregular English past tenses such as *gave* can no longer be further decomposed into a verb root and a past-tense ending, but the same cannot be said for irregularly inflected French verbs, as even the most idiosyncratic roots are inflected for a given tense with the same endings as those used to mark that tense with all other French verbs. This point is potentially of great significance; it suggests that in the case of French, irregular verbs may not be an ecologically valid operationalization of the "words" part of words and rules theory. Differently stated, in contrast to English, the French (and Italian) verbal systems may operate only by "rules."

III
Priming with Inflected French Verbs

The results of Meunier and Marslen-Wilson (2000) and Royle, Jarema, and Kehayia (2002) suggest that French-speaking adults show priming from both regular and irregular French verbs. Given the unexpected nature of these results and their significance for dual-mechanism models of language processing, it is important to attempt to replicate their findings. It is important, too, to note that while at least one of these studies (Meunier and Marslen-Wilson, 2000) was interpreted as supporting the applicability of a dual-mechanism model to lexical representation in French, their results also invite a certain amount of principled speculation, for example, about French-English differences in morphological decomposability, which has already been addressed.

A methodological feature of the Royle, Jarema, and Kehayia study may bear consideration. It is true that the results with their controls converged with the results of Meunier and Marslen-Wilson (2000). However, it is also the case that their results were obtained using a different variation of the priming paradigm than the one used by Meunier and Marslen-Wilson. In the Royle study, primes were presented for durations of two hundred milliseconds followed by a thirty-millisecond interval of blank screen; targets then followed the blank screen and remained on-screen until a subject made a response. By contrast, in their masked-priming experiment, Meunier and Marslen-Wilson presented their primes for much shorter periods of time (forty-seven milliseconds); primes were immediately followed by targets, which were displayed for five hundred milliseconds. Since they were presented for such short durations, these primes were almost certainly not consciously perceived by their subjects. Assuming this is true (and bearing in mind their finding of no priming effects in their control conditions), the pattern of responses observed by Meunier and Marslen-Wilson very likely reflected true morphological-priming effects. Owing to the duration of the visual primes, however, the same cannot be said of the pattern of responses in the Royle study; at two hundred milliseconds in duration, the priming events in their study may well have been consciously perceived. If primes are consciously perceived, and if they are not presented cross-modally, then there is no guarantee that any of the observed priming effects have a uniquely morphological source (cf. Forster and Davis, 1984, as well as the earlier discussion of masked priming). Because they were testing both normals and DLI subjects, the Royle team may have used the longer prime durations to insure that their DLI subjects would show some kind of priming effects. Royle, Jarema, and Kehayia observed similar results from their controls with a simple lexical-decision experiment, and they were able to separate effects of morphological priming from effects of orthographic priming. Thanks to their careful procedures, they very likely did capture genuine morphological-priming effects. Still, in light of the long durations of their primes, it may not be desirable to consider the results of Royle, Jarema, and Kehayia with those of Meunier and Marslen-Wilson. In order to obtain a more balanced picture of how a dual-mechanism model of lexical representation might work in French, the present experiment will revisit the question of morphological processing with French regular and irregular verbs.

In light of the studies by Meunier and Marslen-Wilson and Royle, Jarema, and Kehayia, it was decided to adopt the main design elements of Meunier and Marslen-Wilson (2000) for the present study. As the subjects of this study were not drawn from DLI, Specific Language Impairment (SLI), or other similar populations, primes were presented for a duration similar to that used by Meunier and Marslen-Wilson, specifically fifty-five milliseconds. For most people, such short stimulus-onset asynchronies (SOAs) are below the threshold of conscious awareness; if they lead to priming effects, such masked primes are usually thought to tap morphological processing with little or no contamination from episodic effects or other sources of priming such as associative information (see, e.g., Frost, Forster, and Deutsch, 1997).

Because French listeners are assumed to be sensitive to the internal morphological composition of complex French words, and because the items in this experiment may not exhibit a suitable contrast in morphological productivity (as noted earlier, unlike English verbs, both regular and irregular French verbs use the same highly regular and highly productive inflectional paradigm), it is possible to imagine a result in which priming is observed between both morphologically regular and morphologically irregular French verbs and their infinitival forms. Such a result would constitute a successful replication of Meunier and Marslen-Wilson's 2000 study and be in line with the findings from the controls of Royle, Jarema, and Kehayia, 2002. Furthermore, with the findings and conclusions of Meunier and Marslen-Wilson, such a result would be interpreted as partially supporting a dual-mechanism approach to lexical representation in French.

Why would a successful replication of Meunier and Marslen-Wilson, 2000, constitute only partial support for words and rules theory, when those authors concluded that their results were in line with a dual-mechanism account? I posit that full support for a dual-mechanism approach would require establishing the existence of "words," or irregular, idiosyncratic, or unproductive morphological items in French, without which a crucial half of the dual-mechanism model remains unaccounted for. A full test of productive versus unproductive French morphology will be undertaken in the next chapter. The present experiment, in which both regular and irregular French verbs are tested, should be seen as a methodological backdrop to the next chapter. My reasoning is as follows. While there is both paradigmatic and behavioral evidence that in contrast to English, the French verbal system is highly or even exclusively regular in its inflectional processes, strictly speaking there has been only one study that has offered positive evidence to that effect using a methodology largely viewed as resistant to episodic and associative effects (Meunier and Marslen-Wilson, 2000). This being the case, replication studies are certainly called for. The present study thus seeks to replicate the finding of Meunier and Marslen-Wilson using methods similar to theirs, albeit with different participants and slightly different items. If despite these differences we are able to observe a pattern of responses suggesting rule-based processing for both regular and irregular French verbs, then we will be in the position of knowing exactly what that rule-based pattern looks like when it is obtained with my particular methods. We will then of course also be in the position of being able to see exactly when the rule-based pattern fails to emerge; this will become of crucial importance in the experiment reported in the next chapter, which will use productively and unproductively suffixed French *nouns* instead of regular and irregular verbs. Because the same procedure will be used in both experiments, we will be able to see exactly what effects, if any, result from exchanging items reflecting regularity contrasts for items reflecting productivity contrasts.

Experiment 1: Primed Lexical Decision with Inflected French Verbs

This experiment was designed to investigate whether an inflected French verb will prime its root form, and whether the priming effect is dependent upon a verb's regularity. Degree of priming was also compared with results from an identical-priming condition and two control conditions.

METHOD
Participants

Twenty-four native speakers of French between the ages of twenty-five and forty-one (mean = 32.5 years of age) with normal or corrected-to-normal vision participated in the experiment. Subjects were tested in both France and the United States, at the University of Oregon and at the University of Illinois at Urbana-Champaign.

Stimuli

Test items included the fifty-six verbs of Royle, Jarema, and Kehayia, 2002 (see the appendix for a listing of the stimuli used in this and the other experiments reported in this book). Following their study, these verbs were grouped into four lists of fourteen verbs each: frequent regular verbs, frequent irregular verbs, infrequent regular verbs, and infrequent irregular verbs. Regular verbs consisted of regularly conjugated *-er* verbs with no internal spelling changes. Irregular verbs consisted of irregularly conjugated *-ir, -oir,* and *-re* verbs, in effect collapsing the subcategories of irregular verbs used by Meunier and Marslen-Wilson (2000). Because they found no relation between type of irregularity and degree of priming, for this experiment it was decided to consider all irregulars together. The present design is taken from Royle, Jarema, and Kehayia, 2000, so it deviates from Meunier and Marslen-Wilson's design in that it features a frequency contrast.[6] For a list of verbs taken from Royle, Jarema, and Kehayia, 2000, and used in experiment 1, see the appendix. (The verbs are organized by category, according to regularity and frequency. Item frequency varied in that the high and low frequencies within the groups of both regular and irregular verbs differed on average by a factor of ten.)

Note, however, that no frequency-based analyses were conducted either for this study or for the studies in the following chapters. There are several reasons for this. First of all, while for the verb-based studies there were a sufficient number of regular and irregular verbs to choose from so that some form of contrast in surface frequency could be made, the same cannot be said for the noun-based studies that follow. In these noun studies, the factor of regularity was exchanged with the factor of suffixal productivity. In the case of the unproductively suffixed nouns, there were so few possible items to begin with that controlling for their surface frequency was impossible.

A second reason for not conducting frequency-based analyses is related to the use of priming paradigms in the present studies. Frequency effects, that is, changes in a dependent measure (such as RT to a lexical decision or to naming a word) that vary as a function of the frequency of occurrence of a linguistic item, are most readily detected and straightforwardly interpreted in tasks such as simple (i.e., unprimed) lexical decision, or deciding whether a string of letters is a word. Such tasks are thought to encourage participants to conduct unbiased, full memory-searches. When a prime precedes a stimulus item in a lexical-decision task, the memory search for the item can be biased by the prime. In other words, because the system has been primed to respond, memory may not be fully searched (i.e., the search may be "short-cutted" because of the prime), and as a result, frequency effects such as those observed in unprimed lexical-decision tasks may either be greatly attenuated or fail to surface at all in the primed variant of the task. In any case, my decision to use primed lexical-decision tasks was prompted by the repeated finding in the literature that priming effects only emerge between regularly inflected items.[7] The results of my experiments will therefore focus upon the presence or absence of any such priming effects.[8]

This experiment included five masked-priming conditions: two critical, two control, and one nonce-word condition. In all five conditions, primes were presented in lowercase letters, while stimulus items were presented in uppercase letters. Stimuli were always the infinitival forms of verbs.

In the first critical priming-condition, the identical-priming condition, both regular and irregular primes and stimulus items were identical, for example, *parler*-PARLER (speak-

SPEAK). In the second critical priming-condition, the morphological-priming condition, primes and stimuli were morphologically related, for example, *parlons*-PARLER (we/let us speak-SPEAK) or *parle*-PARLER (he/she/it speaks-SPEAK). There were two control priming-conditions. In the first, the frequency- or length-matched priming condition, stimuli were paired with frequency- and length-matched but orthographically and morphologically unrelated primes, for example, *basons*-PARLER (we/let us base-SPEAK), while in the second, the orthographic-priming condition, primes and stimuli were orthographically but not morphologically related, for example, *partir*-PARLER (leave-SPEAK). In this condition, primes and stimuli were roughly the same length and differed by no more than two or three letters. Finally, there was a nonce, or nonword, condition in which nonword stimuli that resembled possible French words followed real French-word primes, for example, *levier*-*CRALSER, where the asterisk denotes a nonword.

Critical and control items were counterbalanced across four lists such that a given prime was followed by (1) an identical stimulus in one list, (2) a morphologically related stimulus in a second list, (3) a frequency- and length-matched control word in a third list, and (4) an orthographically related control in a fourth list. In each list, there were a total of eighty-four real-word trials (fifty-six critical and twenty-eight control trials). Together with eighty-four nonce trials, this resulted in a total of 168 trials in each list.

PROCEDURE

Subjects were tested individually in a quiet room. Written instructions specified that subjects would be making decisions about letter strings that would appear on their computer screen. The instructions specified that while some letter strings would be legitimate French words (e.g., *manger*), others would not be (e.g., **malger*). Subjects were told that each string would be preceded by a row of pound signs (########), and that the pound signs would be replaced by letter strings. As soon as the letter string appeared, subjects were to press the YES trigger of a response pad if they thought the string was a French word, or the NO trigger if they did not think the letter string was a French word. A short training period with feedback on accuracy and RT preceded the actual experiment. No feedback was provided during the experiment. The instructions emphasized both speed and accuracy in responding.[9]

Trials began with a five-hundred-millisecond pause, followed by the display of a row of pound signs (######) at the center of the computer screen. The pound signs remained on screen for five hundred milliseconds, after which two events occurred in immediate succession: (1) the pound signs were replaced by a prime word, which was displayed for fifty-five milliseconds and (2) the prime word was in turn replaced by a stimulus word, which remained on screen for five hundred milliseconds. Participants had two seconds to respond, after which time the next trial automatically began. The order in which items were presented was randomized for each participant.

PREDICTIONS

If the results of previous studies can be generalized and both regular and irregular French verbs prime their infinitives, then given this study's design and procedure we should observe the following results:

1. No effect of regularity, that is, a nonsignificant difference (nsd) in RTs to lexical decisions for regular and irregular verbs
2. No interaction between regularity and priming condition
3. A nsd in RTs to lexical decisions between the identical- and morphological-priming conditions, that is, for all regular and irregular verbs, RTs in the identical-priming condition should be statistically inseparable from RTs in the morphological-priming condition
4. Faster RTs in the identical- and morphological-priming conditions than in the two control priming-conditions, that is, both identical and morphological priming should be superior to priming with controls

RESULTS

Errors, which constituted less than 1 percent of the data, were removed prior to analysis. RTs that were less than one hundred milliseconds and greater than fifteen hundred milliseconds were also removed. This resulted in a loss of 2.7 percent of the data.

RT data tend to be positively skewed because while there is a lower limit to response time in that a person cannot respond faster than in zero milliseconds, there is potentially no upper limit to how long someone can take to respond. To reduce positive skew for this and subsequent experiments, I performed reciprocal transformations on the RT data (i.e., inverse transformations, as in 1/RT) prior to statistical analysis (Ratcliff, 1993). Mean RTs, standard deviations, and standard errors

Table 3.1. Mean RT (ms.) according to priming condition, for experiment 1

	Mean RT	Std. Dev.	Std. Err.
Control	644	90.1	18.4
Identical	580	109.9	22.4
Morphological	590	90.4	18.5
1st Plural	617	79	16.1
3rd Singular	596	108.3	22.1
Regular	606	89.9	18.3
Irregular	598	94.3	19.2
Orthographic	623	128.8	26.3

are presented by condition in table 3.1. In this experiment and in those that follow, the descriptive statistics provided are from the untransformed data.

An ANOVA with the between-subjects factor of list failed to reach significance ($p < .3$).[10] Following this initial analysis, all lists were combined for the analyses described below.

An ANOVA with the within-subjects factor of priming condition (frequency- and length-matched control vs. identical- vs. morphological- vs. orthographic-priming conditions) revealed a significant RT difference between the four levels of priming type ($F_{(3, 23)} = 11.29$, $p < .0001$). Planned comparisons revealed that while the ten-millisecond RT difference between the morphological- and identical-priming conditions failed to reach significance ($t_{(23)} = -1.12$, $p = .27$), both the 64-millisecond RT difference between the control and identical-priming conditions and the fifty-four-millisecond RT difference between the control and morphological-priming conditions were significant ($t_{(23)} = 4.24$, $p = .0003$, and $t_{(23)} = 5.26$, $p < .0001$, respectively). Also, while the twenty-one-millisecond

RT difference between the orthographic-priming condition and frequency- and length-matched control priming-condition failed to reach significance ($t(23) = 1.34, p = .19$), both the forty-three-millisecond RT difference between the orthographic- and identical-priming conditions and the thirty-three-millisecond RT difference between the orthographic- and morphological-priming conditions did reach significance ($t(23) = 3.24, p = .003$, and $t(23) = 2.34, p = .02$, respectively).

A second ANOVA with the within-subjects factor of prime inflection-type (frequency- and length-matched control vs. identical vs. third person singular vs. first person plural) revealed a significant difference among the four levels of inflection type ($F(3, 23) = 12.15, p < .0001$). Planned comparisons revealed that the sixty-three-millisecond advantage for identical primes over control words was significant ($t(23) = 4.24, p = .0003$). Likewise, the forty-seven-millisecond advantage for third-person-singular primes over control words was significant ($t(23) = 3.55, p = .0017$), as was the twenty-six-millisecond advantage of first-person-plural primes over control words ($t(23) = 4.92, p < .0001$). The thirty-six-millisecond advantage of identical primes over third-person-plural primes also proved to be significant ($t(23) = 3.18, p = .004$), as did the twenty-millisecond advantage for third-person-singular primes over first-person-plural primes ($t(23) = 1.99, p = .05$). However, the fifteen-millisecond advantage for identical primes over third-person-singular primes just missed significance ($t(23) = 1.89, p = .07$).

A third ANOVA with the within-subjects factor of regularity (frequency- and length-matched control vs. regular verbs vs. irregular verbs) revealed significant differences among the three levels of regularity ($F(2, 23) = 15.39, p < .0001$). Planned comparisons showed that while the eight-millisecond RT advantage for irregulars over regulars was not significant ($p = .28$), the forty-six-millisecond advantage for irregulars over controls and the thirty-eight-millisecond advantage for regulars over controls were both significant ($t\,(23) = -4.44$, $p = .0002$, and $t\,(23) = -4.27$, $p = .0003$, respectively).

A final ANOVA with the within-subjects factors of priming condition and regularity failed to reveal an interaction between these two factors ($p < .2$).

Conclusion

The results of the present experiment suggest that for native French-speaking adults, inflected forms of French verbs are as effective as identical primes at priming their infinitival forms. What is more, both regular and irregular forms of inflected French verbs prime their infinitival forms better than length- and frequency-matched controls. Yet regular and irregular verbs do not differ in the degree to which they prime their infinitival forms. Further findings from the present experiment show that both third-person-plural and first-person-singular inflected verb-forms are effective primes. However, first-person-plural inflected forms are not as effective at priming their infinitival forms as are third-person-singular inflected forms (in this experiment, the latter are as effective as identical primes).

These results constitute a successful replication of the results of Meunier and Marslen-Wilson, 2000. Using different items and testing different participants, the present study showed that both regular and irregular French verbs are equally efficacious primes for their infinitival forms. Put differently, we now have independent confirmation that in contrast to English, the inflection of French regular and irregular verbs proceeds on the basis of rules.

However, it would be premature to conclude on the basis of this finding that a dual-mechanism model adequately accounts for lexical representation in French. As I noted earlier, we still need to find evidence of "words" in French, that is, items that, similar to English irregular past-tense forms, are not processed on the basis of rules but instead are stored in and recalled from memory. But because both regular and irregular verbs in French are processed with rules this means that, again in contrast to the case of English, we are obliged to look elsewhere in the French language for our "words." To find such items, I propose the following. First, that in the case of French, the crucial distinction with respect to dual-mechanism models concerns not regularity, but *productivity*, in particular suffixal productivity. As Meunier and Marslen-Wilson (2000) noted, irrespective of regularity, all French verbs use the same inflectional suffixes, that is, there are no instances in the inflectional system of French verbs that are similar to the case of the English irregular past tense, in that certain inflectional forms represent long-dead, or synchronically unproductive, morphological processes. Second, that in order to find items that contrast in suffixal productivity, it is necessary to consider items other than verbs; as we have seen, the contrast does not exist in the French inflectional system. However, as we will see in the next experiment, it does exist in the French *derivational* system.

IV

From French Rules
to French Words

The study by Meunier and Marslen-Wilson (2000) is of great interest in that it examined the mental representation of regular and irregular French verbs using methodologies that when used previously with English speakers, had shown support for dual-mechanism accounts such as words and rules theory. Given that the materials tested reflected a contrast in French verb-paradigm regularity similar to that found with English regular and irregular past-tense forms, a reasonable expectation was that the French participants of Meunier and Marslen-Wilson's study, like the English subjects in previous studies, would show evidence of morphological priming only with materials drawn from regular verbs. As we saw, however, this is not what was found. Instead, it was observed that French participants showed equally strong morphological priming with materials drawn from both regular and irregular verbs. The most straightforward interpretation of such a finding is the one that Meunier and Marslen-Wilson adopted: both regular and irregular French verbs are processed using rules. Similar findings were reported by Royle, Jarema, and Kehayia (2002). In the primed lexical-decision experiment reported in that study, a francophone Canadian control group also showed no effect of regularity: both regular and irregular verbs showed equal effects of morphological priming. The experiment in the previous chapter, which used a primed lexical-decision task similar to the one described in Meunier and Marslen-Wilson, 2000, and tested regular and irregular French verbs from Royle, Jarema, and Kehayia, 2002, also showed equally strong priming effects with both regular and irregular inflected French verbs. Taken together, these findings constitute compelling evidence that the French verbal system contrasts with the English verbal system in that the French system overwhelmingly relies upon rules for the representation and processing of both regular and irregular verbs. In fact, the relatively high degree of inflectional regularity in French may mean that French speakers have little choice but to rely upon rules for the processing of both regular and irregular inflected French verbs.

In the context of words and rules theory, however, this conclusion leaves an unanswered question: where are the "words"? That is, where is the evidence for morphological items in French that have been learned associatively, or by rote? Meunier and Marslen-Wilson considered but rejected as implausible a single-mechanism account of their results, yet their results provided evidence only of rule-based processing. While Royle, Jarema, and Kehayia did not directly address this in their study, their results and the results of my chapter 3 experiment lead to the same question.

Where else in the French language should we look for the existence of morphologically complex items that are not computed using rules but are stored or listed as whole entities in the minds of French speakers? A potential clue might lie in a notion that is related to morphological decomposability, namely, morphological productivity, or the degree to which a morphological pattern generalizes to new forms. How might these two notions be related? One possible way of characterizing the relationship between morphological decomposability and morphological productivity is the following: morphological decomposability pertains to individual language users and the extent to which a given person or group of persons may be conscious of the morphemic structure of some words in their language but not others, whereas morphological productivity pertains to corpora, dictionaries, or other aggregated language samples and the extent to which language features such as morphemic structure are present within them. Clearly, the two concepts are closely related in that they both concern language features and language users. In the case of morphological decomposability, it is the language user who is central. By reversing figure and ground and making language features central, we arrive at the concept of morphological productivity.

There is another sense in which there would appear to be a close relationship between morphological decomposability and morphological productivity: in order for a morphological feature to be productive, the feature must in some sense be "visible," that is, recoverable through decomposition by speakers of a language. Relatedly, if speakers of a language are no longer able to decompose a morphologically complex item into its component morphemes, then the components of that item should demonstrate reduced productivity. Pinker and colleagues have implicated productivity as a factor distinguishing regular and irregular past-tense English verb formation (Pinker, 2000; Pinker and Ullman, 2002). For example, while speakers of a language will by default apply the regular past-tense suffix -*ed* to novel verb forms, speakers will only seldom generalize irregular past-tense forms. Meunier and Marslen-Wilson (2000) noted that unlike English irregular past tenses, French irregular verbs are decomposable. To the extent that decomposability and productivity are related, this implies that regular and irregular French verbs, unlike English verbs, do not include a contrast in morphological decomposability or productivity; therefore, research investigating the processing of French regular and irregular verbs will fail to find evidence of a behavioral distinction that would support a dual-mechanism model of lexical representation. I hold that this difference in the representation of regular and irregular verbs in French and English is the source of the results reported in Meunier and Marslen-Wilson, 2000; Royle, Jarema, and Kehayia, 2002; and my experiment in the previous chapter. In each case, there was no behavioral dissociation observed because for the items tested, there was no morphological opposition between productive and decomposable on the one hand, and unproductive and undecomposable on the other.

If the French verb inflectional system does not embody the crucial contrasts in morphological decomposability and morphological productivity that English does such that some items are the product of rules while others are the product of associative, or rote, learning, are there such contrasts elsewhere in the language? Below, we will see that there are in fact morphological items in French that bear the crucial contrast. However, the items in question are not verb inflections but rather derivational morphemes.

From Inflections to French Derivational Suffixes

Up until now, the studies we have considered have all been concerned with the processing of inflectional morphology in one language or another. Inflectional morphology concerns differences in English words such as *walked* and *walks,* or in French words such as *marché* and *marches:* with both the English and French words, there are inflectional suffixes (i.e., *-ed, -s* and *-é, -s*) that are added onto a base or root form of a verb and that denote grammatical information, in this case information pertaining to tense and number. These and other inflectional suffixes have been said to bear *morphosyntactic information* in that they interact both with the word or root they attach to and with the words surrounding them in a sentence (Matthews, 1974). In many languages, including French and (to a lesser extent, as we have seen) English, inflectional morphology is highly productive in that it typically applies across the board to all eligible items (e.g., the third-person-singular *-s,* which applies indiscriminately to all present-tense indicative English verbs). An additional feature of inflectional morphology concerns its class-maintaining status; for instance, adding the suffix *-ed* to the verb *walk* does not result in *walk*'s changing from a verb to some other lexical category. A final feature of inflectional morphology is that it is considered to be *closed,* that is, synchronically speaking there are no new grammatical categories being created within a given language either by suffixation or by any other morphological process.

The flip side of inflectional morphology is derivational morphology. If inflectional morphological processes can be characterized as processes by which morphosyntactic information pertaining to tense, mood, aspect, number, and gender is indicated for nouns and verbs, then derivational morphological processes can be characterized as processes relating to the structure of existing words and the formation of new ones. For example, in English, the noun *driver* is formed through the morphological process of adding the derivational suffix *-er* to the verb *drive*. This same morphological process gives us many other nouns such as *painter, teacher,* and so forth, all of which have the same structure as *driver.*

In my view, models of lexical representation and morphological processing should strive to account for the processing of both inflectional and derivational morphology. Possibly because the groundbreaking work was done with English regular and irregular past tenses (Pinker and Prince, 1988; Rumelhart and McClelland, 1986), subsequent studies have largely focused upon the mental representation of inflected verbs in different languages, with (as we have seen) mixed results in the case of Romance languages. But what about derivational morphology? It is, after all, a type of morphology, just one that primarily has scope over word formation, according to some researchers, through the application of rules of word-formation that are not part of the grammar but are a property of the lexicon (cf. the earlier discussion of words and rules theory's view of irregular English verbs). Current understanding of the processing distinction underlying the words-rules dichotomy is that it is not crucially tied to inflections; instead, it represents two mental processes, one of which is concerned with creating language items through combining elements, while the other is largely dependent upon storing and retrieving language items from memory. The English regular past tense represents item creation through combination, and the English irregular past tense represents item creation through storage and retrieval. The French verb system, it seems, represents item creation only through combination. Assuming (as I do) the universal viability of words and rules theory, this suggests that a words-rules distinction should be found somewhere else within the French language. I therefore propose the following: to the extent that word-formation and derivational processes

can, like inflectional processes, be characterized in terms of
rules that are to varying degrees productive, the study of derivational processes represents a natural extension from existing studies of lexical representation and processing. For this
reason, I propose switching attention from French verbs to
French words, that is, from inflections to derivations. If it can
be shown that French derivational morphology includes productivity contrasts similar to the regular-irregular past-tense-
inflection productivity contrast of English, and that these contrasts in derivational productivity have processing relevance
for speakers of French, such findings would constitute strong
evidence in favor of a dual-mechanism account of lexical representation in French.

Some Differences between Inflectional and Derivational Morphology

What are some of the differences between inflectional and derivational morphology? For example, consider the morphologically complex English word *unbelievable* or the morphologically complex French word *incroyable.* These words were
formed through the addition of derivational affixes (*un-* and
-able, in- and *-able,* respectively) to base or root forms of other
words according to the rules of word formation in English and
French. Unlike inflectional morphology, derivational morphology usually signals a change in grammatical class for the root
or base form. For instance, the root or base form of *unbelievable* is a verb, *believe;* depending upon its use in a sentence, *unbelievable* (the derived form) is either a noun or an adjective.
In another contrast to inflectional morphology, derivational
morphology may not always be productive or regular in meaning because while some derivational morphemes are highly

productive (e.g., the suffix -*ism* in English), others do not indiscriminately combine with all possible root or base forms (e.g., the suffix -*ity*, which combines with rapid to form *rapidity*, but does not combine with *sad* to form **sadity*). Furthermore, in different words the same suffix can sometimes give rise to unpredictable meanings (e.g., *hateful* means "full of hate," yet *spoonful* does not mean "full of spoons").

A final, related contrast concerns the notions of morphological productivity and decomposability. As we have seen, derivational morphology varies in its productivity, and this implies that there are differences in the degree to which individuals can "see into" the morphological structure of complex derived words. By way of example, consider the English words *prioritize* and *neighborhood*. Both words are derived from nouns: the first from *priority*, to which a derivational suffix, -*ize*, has been added, and the second from *neighbor*, to which a different derivational suffix, -*hood*, has been added. These two suffixes vary in their productivity in that while there are many other -*ize* verbs derived from nouns (e.g., *alphabetize, animalize, atomize, baptize, bastardize*, etc.), there seem to be rather fewer -*hood* nouns derived from nouns. Moreover, even if individuals have difficulty defining the meaning of the derivational suffix -*ize*, most people if asked would likely express an awareness of the suffix -*ize* as a distinct morphological entity because it appears in many English words and is used to form new English verbs. The same cannot be said for the derivational suffix -*hood*; its restricted productivity suggests that individuals would be less likely to be aware of it as a distinct morphological entity and would therefore be less willing to form new English words using it.

So far, we have been talking in intuitive terms about variations in the productivity of derivational morphemes. With access to sufficiently large language corpora there are, however, more exact ways of quantifying morphological productivity. For instance, using large corpora containing many millions of words, Baayen and colleagues have elaborated a quantitative approach to morphological productivity (Baayen, 1992; Baayen and Lieber, 1991). Very briefly, such an approach expresses morphological productivity as the likelihood or probability of encountering a word with a given suffix once a certain amount of a (sufficiently large) text is sampled. Such estimates of probability hinge crucially upon (1) the total number of words ending in a given suffix and (2) the number of hapax legomena, or words bearing that suffix that appear only once within a corpus.

Another way to proceed with quantifying morphological productivity is to track the number of words bearing a particular suffix over time within different editions of the same dictionary (cf. Anshen and Aronoff, 1999). For example, the Académie Française, a learned society that has been charged with preparing a French grammar and dictionary since 1635, has published several editions of its dictionary over the course of its nearly 370 years of existence. By searching different editions of the dictionary and tallying in each one the number of words bearing a given derivational suffix, a longitudinal picture of that suffix's productivity will emerge.

Clearly, there are advantages and disadvantages to both approaches to quantifying suffixal productivity. In the case of large corpora of written (or spoken) discourse produced by and intended for native speakers of a language, the data have a high ecological validity in that they likely represent the spontaneous or planned discourse of potentially many different speakers. However, it is important to have a large corpus; if the corpus is not large enough (i.e., in the many millions of words), then there is a risk of sampling errors of various kinds (for instance,

the frequencies of infrequent words are likely to be underesti-
mated; Gernsbacher, 1984). Regarding the use of different editions of the same dictionary, in this case different editions of
the dictionary of the Académie Française, the data have far less
ecological validity in that, strictly speaking, they represent not
the language of potentially many speakers, but committee decisions as to which words should or should not be included in
the dictionary. A normative, committee-designed dictionary
might therefore be less than ideal for tracking the ebb and flow
of suffixal use in what some might view as nonstandard French
and which might not be included in an official dictionary of
the language. In fact, prior to the 1832-35 edition, the Académie
purposely excluded scientific and technical terms from their
dictionary. However, different editions of such a dictionary
should still be suitable for establishing approximate longitudinal measures of suffixal productivity within standard French.

In the present study, for the purpose of identifying both
productive and unproductive derivational suffixes, I will draw
primarily upon the dictionary-based method. I will also supplement the dictionary data with corpus data. Fortunately, the
issue of identifying possible productive and unproductive
French derivational suffixes was addressed in an earlier study
of derivational morphology in French (Dubois, 1962; for related
discussion, see Dubois and Dubois-Charlier, 1999 and Thiele,
1987; for a discussion of morphological productivity, see Bauer,
2001).

A Study of French Derivational
Morphology: Dubois, 1962

Most available studies of the derivational morphology of
French are limited in that they were conducted before the ad-

vent of cheap, powerful computing resources and digitized, freely accessible dictionaries. For example, in his study of the productivity of French derivational morphology, Dubois (1962) compared two paper versions (1906 and 1961) of the *Petit Larousse*. Because of the sheer number of entries in these dictionaries (over 80,000 total entries, according to Dubois), Dubois limited his inquiry to words beginning with the letter A in both editions of the dictionary.

For my purposes, Dubois' study seemed somewhat limited in scope. However, in examining his sample of the two editions of the *Petit Larousse*, Dubois did elaborate three indices that allowed him—and subsequently me—to quantify the degree of change in productivity over time for a given suffix within different versions of the same dictionary. Specifically, Dubois identified three ways of tracking the vitality of a given suffix:

1. coefficient of mobility: this is the proportion of the total number of words ending in a particular suffix recorded in different editions of the same dictionary to the total number of such words gained and lost between different editions
2. coefficient of recession: this is the proportion of the number of words ending in a particular suffix recorded in the earliest edition of a dictionary to the number of such words lost between the earliest and last editions of that dictionary
3. coefficient of expansion: this is the proportion of the number of words ending in a particular suffix recorded in the last edition of a dictionary to the number of such words added since the first edition of that dictionary

The French Derivational Suffixes -*isme* and -*té*

According to Dubois (1962, p. 25), if the coefficient of mobility for a suffix falls below 10 percent, the suffix is no longer perceived as available and is typically no longer used to produce new suffixed words. Likewise, if the coefficient of expansion for a given suffix is high, this indicates that that suffix is increasingly being used to create new words. Dubois asserted, albeit without coefficient support (possibly because this suffix was found in too few words within the letter A to provide meaningful figures; see p. 27 of Dubois for discussion), that among the less mobile suffixes used to create nouns between the 1906 and 1961 editions of the *Petit Larousse,* the suffix -*té* (a variant of the suffix -*ité;* both mean roughly "having the quality of") had become all but lexicalized. He further notes (p. 35) that for the suffix -*isme,* the coefficients of mobility and expansion were so high (32.2 and 41.8, respectively) as to strongly suggest that the suffix was being used to coin new words in all domains. Searches of the *Trésor de la Langue Française Informatisé* (at http://atilf.atilf.fr/tlf.htm) revealed that approximately 180 words across diverse domains bore the suffix -*isme;* far fewer words (approximately 40) ended in -*té.* Furthermore, in contrast to other less productive or unproductive suffixes such as -*iot,* -*ure,* and -*aison,* the suffix -*té* was suffixed to a sufficient number of nouns to allow for the design of both word- and sentence-level studies. Therefore, it was decided to apply Dubois' methodology to larger, more-modern databases and to use the suffixes -*isme* and -*té* to further explore lexical representation and processing in French speakers.

At the time this study was being planned, the *Dictionnaires de l'Académie Française* pages of the American and French Research on the Treasury of the French Language (ARTFL)

Table 4.1. Number of lexical entries for nouns ending in -*té* and -*isme,* by year

	1694	1798	1835	1932−35
-*té*	51	49	51	46
-*isme*	26	122	156	306

Source: http://www.lib.uchicago.edu/efts/ARTFL/projects/dicos/ACADEMIE

Project (at http://www.lib.uchicago.edu/efts/ARTFL/projects/dicos/ACADEMIE/) offered online versions of the first, fifth, sixth, and eighth editions of the dictionary of the Académie Française. ARTFL subscribers can access both headwords and full text for all editions of the Académie dictionary. These different editions include the years 1694, 1798, 1835, and 1932−35. Insofar as they represent the same scope and aims from one edition to the next, the different editions of the Académie dictionary can provide the longitudinal data to which Dubois' indices of morphological growth and decline can be applied.

Accordingly, I searched the Académie dictionaries for nouns ending in -*isme* and -*té;* these were hand tallied and sorted by year. Table 4.1 represents the total number of lexical entries for nouns ending in -*té* and -*isme* by year, and table 4.2 represents the number of lexical items gained and lost for nouns ending in -*té* and -*isme* by period of years.

Applying Dubois' methodology to this larger database yields coefficient values that are largely consistent with the assertions he made based upon his much smaller sample: nouns with a suffix of -*té* have a coefficient of mobility of approximately 12.5 percent, whereas nouns ending in -*isme* have a coefficient of mobility of almost 53 percent. Thus, the data from tables 4.1 and 4.2 suggest that there have been a greater number of new word formations in French with the suffix -*isme*

Table 4.2 Number of lexical items gained and lost for nouns ending in -té and -isme, by period of years

	1694–1798		1798–1835		1835–1932/35	
	gained	lost	gained	lost	gained	lost
-té	6	8	2	0	2	7
-isme	71	0	40	3	180	32

Source: http://www.lib.uchicago.edu/efts/ARTFL/projects/dicos/ACADEMIE

than with the suffix -té. This seems particularly evident upon inspection of table 4.2, where it can be seen that the number and ratio of words gained and lost during the period from 1835 to 1932–35 is greatly skewed in favor of -isme.

In order to supplement the dictionary analyses, I also decided to find and examine a French corpus. The requirements were that the corpus be relatively large (at least several million words), be searchable, and comprise a variety of different kinds of discourse. Few corpora of transcribed spoken French data exist, and of those that are available, none are in the public domain. However, the Frantext archive, available to ARTFL subscribers (at http://www.lib.uchicago.edu/efts/ARTFL/databases/TLF/), offers a truly voluminous repository of a variety of forms of written French discourse. The texts, dating from the Renaissance through approximately 1960, include almost two thousand novels, verses, theater pieces, newspaper articles, essays, correspondence, and treatises. Subjects covered include literary criticism, biology, history, economics, and philosophy. In all, the Frantext archive includes over 114,000,000 words with 400,000 unique forms.

Following in the tradition of corpus work outlined earlier (Baayen and colleagues), I searched the Frantext database for nouns ending in *-té* and *-isme,* noting the total number of occurrences as well as the total number of hapax words for nouns ending in both suffixes. Ideally, the corpus data should demonstrate that a reader is more likely to encounter a novel noun with *-isme* than with *-té,* that is, the corpus data should converge with the dictionary data that suggested that *-isme* is a more productive suffix than *-té.* Following an inspection of the raw search results, which led to a small percentage of misspelled items being discarded, the searches of Frantext revealed 13,011 nouns suffixed with *-té,* of which 48 were hapax words, and 37,157 nouns suffixed with *-isme,* of which 298 were hapax words. According to Baayen and colleagues' reasoning, this means that the probability of encountering an *-isme* noun ($p = .0080$) is in fact numerically greater than the probability of encountering a *-té* noun ($p = .0036$). Thus, both the dictionary data and the corpus data converged in support of Dubois, 1962, suggesting that the suffix *-isme* is in fact more productive than the suffix *-té.* This convergence should have a processing consequence: if the source of the productivity differences between the French derivational suffixes *-isme* and *-té* ultimately lies in the collective minds of French speakers, as the source of the productivity differences between regular and irregular English past tenses seems to lie in the collective minds of English speakers, then it should be the case that behavioral reflexes reflecting this productivity difference will emerge under controlled conditions. Specifically, we expect that in a primed lexical-decision experiment, speakers of French will show priming effects between *-isme* nouns and their root forms, but they will show no priming effects between *-té* nouns and their root forms.

Experiment 2: Primed Lexical Decision
with Derived French Nouns

This experiment was designed to investigate whether a derived French noun will prime its root form, and whether the priming effect is dependent upon the productivity of the derived noun's suffix. The amount of priming was compared between derived nouns with productive suffixes and their root forms, and derived nouns with less productive suffixes and their root forms. Degree of priming with productively and less productively suffixed nouns was also compared with an identical-priming condition and two control conditions.

METHOD
Participants

Twenty-five native speakers of French between the ages of twenty-four and forty (mean = 30 years of age) with normal or corrected vision took part in the experiment. Subjects were tested in both France and the United States, at the University of Oregon and at the University of Illinois at Urbana-Champaign.

Stimuli

Twenty-four prime-target pairs, with twelve each of nouns ending in *-isme* and *-té*, were selected from the Frantext database.

This experiment included five masked-priming conditions: two critical, two control, and one nonce-word condition. In all five conditions, primes were presented in lowercase letters, while stimulus items were presented in uppercase letters. In accordance with the design of the previous verb experiment, in which stimuli were always the infinitival forms of verbs, stimuli in the present experiment were always the root or base form of a noun. For each derivational suffix type, the following critical priming-conditions were created: in the first, the identical-priming condition, prime-stimulus pairs were identical (e.g., *propre*-PROPRE); in the second, the morphological-priming condition, prime-stimulus pairs were morphologically related (e.g., *propreté*-PROPRE). There were two control priming-conditions. In the first, the frequency- or length-matched condition, primes and stimuli were semantically, orthographically, and morphologically unrelated, but they were matched for surface frequency and as closely as possible in number of letters (e.g., *maline*-PROPRE). In the second, the orthographic-priming condition, items were orthographically but not semantically or morphologically related (e.g., *pourpre*-PROPRE). In this condition, primes and stimuli were roughly the same length and differed by no more than between two and three letters. Finally, in the nonce-word condition, French-word primes were paired with nonword targets (e.g., *maladie*-*BICRONDE).

As before, critical and control items were counterbalanced across four lists such that a given prime was followed by (1) an identical form in one list, (2) a morphologically related (i.e., root) form in a second list, (3) a frequency- and length-matched control word in a third list, and (4) an orthographically related control in a fourth list. In order to have a balanced number of real-word and nonword trials, an additional eighteen trials were created in which French nouns were followed by nonwords. This resulted in twenty-four real-word target trials and twenty-four nonword target trials, for a total of forty-eight trials for each list.

PROCEDURE

Participants were tested individually during a single session in a quiet room. Written instructions specified that each experimental trial would begin with a string of pound signs (###########) appearing across the computer screen, and that the pound signs would be replaced by a string of letters. The instructions specified that while some letter strings would be legitimate French words (e.g., *chien*), others would not be (e.g., *clien). As soon as the letter string appeared, subjects were to press the YES trigger of a response pad if they thought the string was a French word, or the NO trigger if they did not think the letter string was a French word. A short training period with feedback on accuracy and RT preceded the actual experiment. No feedback was provided during the experiment. The instructions emphasized both speed and accuracy in responding. Trials began with a five-hundred-millisecond pause, followed by the display of a row of pound signs at the center of the computer screen. The pound signs remained on screen for five hundred milliseconds, after which two events occurred in immediate succession: (1) the pound signs were replaced by a prime word, which was displayed for approximately fifty-five milliseconds and (2) the prime word was in turn replaced by a stimulus word, which remained on screen for five hundred milliseconds or until the subject pressed a response button. The order in which items were presented was randomized for each subject.

PREDICTIONS

Differences in productivity patterns observed over a 310-year period for the French suffixes *-isme* and *-té* suggest that, synchronically, nouns derived with these suffixes should be differ-

ently represented in the mental lexicon. Specifically, similar to
the English regular past tense, productively derived -*isme*
nouns should tend to be the product of rules (albeit derivational rules rather than inflectional ones). If so, and if speakers
process productively derived items the way they have been
shown to process productively inflected items in both English
and French, then nouns suffixed with -*isme* should prime their
root forms. However, similar to the English irregular past
tense, unproductively derived -*té* nouns should not be the
product of rules but should instead be stored in and retrieved
from memory. If so, and if speakers process unproductively
derived language items the way they have been shown to process unproductively inflected items in English, then there
should be greatly attenuated or even nonexistent priming between nouns suffixed with -*té* and their root forms.

In both experiment 1 and experiment 2, there was an unavoidable confound in that morphologically related items also
bore a form resemblance. In experiment 1, with both regular
and irregular verbs it was possible to statistically distinguish
between purely orthographic priming and identical or morphological priming. For the present experiment, however, I an-
ticipate a slightly different set of findings. In the case of -*isme*
nouns, despite the orthographic-morphological overlap, it
should again be possible to differentiate between morphological and purely orthographic priming because of the productive status of the -*isme* suffix. By contrast, with -*té* nouns, the
dictionary and corpus evidence suggest that they represent
nondecomposable, "frozen" forms; as such, morphological
priming should be greatly reduced with -*té* nouns. This does
not mean, however, that the unavoidable orthographic overlap
in the morphological-priming condition will play no role in
the case of -*té* nouns; rather, I posit that with these nouns, it

will prove difficult if not impossible to statistically distinguish between morphological and purely orthographic priming precisely because in both conditions, responses should still be influenced by orthographic overlap.

Specifically, with our design and procedure we should observe the following:

1. With -*isme* nouns, there should be a nsd in RTs to lexical decisions between the identical- and morphological-priming conditions.

2. With -*isme* nouns, RTs in the identical- and morphological-priming conditions should be faster than in the control priming conditions, that is, both identical- and morphological-priming should be superior to priming with controls.

3. With -*té* nouns, RTs in the identical-priming condition should be faster than in the morphological-priming condition.

4. With -*té* nouns, RTs in the identical-priming condition should be faster than in the control priming-conditions.

5. With -*té* nouns, while there should be a significant difference between the morphological and frequency- or length-matched control priming-conditions, there should be a nsd between the morphological- and orthographic-priming conditions.

If this final prediction is accurate, it would suggest that for nouns suffixed with -*té*, it is not possible to separate the effects of morphological priming from the effects of orthographic priming. Together with the third prediction above, this result would suggest that morphological priming was not a factor for -*té* nouns.

RESULTS

RTs that were greater than fifteen hundred milliseconds were discarded. This resulted in a loss of 2.3 percent of the data. As in experiment 1, to reduce skew while retaining numerical outliers, RTs were inversely transformed prior to statistical analysis. Errors, which constituted 6 percent of the data and which were almost exclusively in the frequency- or length-matched control condition, were also removed from the data.

Two ANOVAs with the within-subjects factor of priming type (frequency- or length-matched control vs. identical vs. morphological vs. orthographic), one for -*té* nouns, the other for -*isme* nouns, were run on the RT data. Mean RTs by condition are presented in table 4.3, while figure 4.1 charts the main results with these items.

For *té*-suffixed nouns, an ANOVA revealed that there was a significant RT difference between the levels of priming type (F (3, 21) = 7.9, p = .0001).[11] Planned comparisons revealed that the 131-millisecond advantage of the identical-priming condition over the frequency- or length-matched control condition was significant (t (21) = 2.29, p = .03), as was the 181-millisecond advantage of the morphological-priming condition over length- or frequency-matched controls (t (21) = 3.24, p = .004) and the 192-millisecond advantage of orthographic priming over frequency- or length-matched controls (t (21) = 3.25, p = .003). Moreover, the 50-millisecond advantage of the morphological-priming condition over the identical-priming condition was significant (t (21) = 2.02, p = .05), as was the 61-millisecond advantage of the orthographic-priming condition

Table 4.3. Repeated measures ANOVA for priming condition, -té suffixed items: $F(3, 21) = 7.9, p = .0001$

Mean RT (ms.) according to Priming Condition:

	Mean RT	Std. Dev.	Std. Err.
Control	812	361.4	77
Identical	681	183.7	39.1
Morphological	631	128.4	27.3
Orthographic	620	109.8	23.4

Planned comparisons:
Control, Morphological: $t(21) = 3.24, p = .004$
Control, Identical: $t(21) = 2.29, p = .03$
Control, Orthographic: $t(21) = 3.25, p = .003$
Identical, Morphological: $t(21) = 2.02, p = .05$
Identical, Orthographic: $t(21) = 2.38, p = .02$
Morphological, Orthographic: $t(21) = .12, p = .9$

over the identical-priming condition ($t(21) = 2.38, p = .02$). However, the 11-millisecond advantage of the orthographic-priming over the morphological-priming condition was in fact not significant ($t(21) = .12, p = .9$).

Turning to the set of *-isme* nouns, a different pattern of results emerges. Mean RTs by condition are charted in table 4.4. Figure 4.2 charts the ANOVA with these items, in which it can be seen that there was a significant RT difference between the levels of priming type ($F(3, 23) = 20.58, p < .0001$).

Planned comparisons reveal that the 90-millisecond advantage of the identical-priming condition over length- or frequency-matched controls was significant ($t(23) = 3.01$,

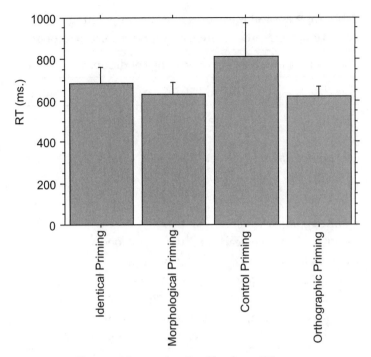

Figure 4.1 Interaction Bar Plot for -*té* Nouns.
Error Bars: 95 Percent Confidence Interval

$p = .006$). The 153-millisecond advantage of the morphological-priming condition over length- or frequency-matched controls was also significant (t (23) = 5.25, $p < .0001$). Moreover, the 63-millisecond advantage of the morphological-priming condition over the identical-priming condition was also significant (t (23) = 2.61, $p = .01$). The results with -*té* nouns showed that while it was possible to separate the effects of identical priming from the effects of orthographic priming, it proved impossible to separate the effects of morphological priming from the effects of orthographic priming. In the present results, however, it is possible to observe a separation be-

Table 4.4. Repeated-measures ANOVA for priming condition, *isme*-suffixed items: $F(3, 23) = 20.58, p < .0001$

Mean RT (ms.) according to priming condition:

	Mean RT	Std. Dev.	Std. Err.
Control	831	247	50.4
Identical	741	210.9	43
Morphological	678	160.2	32.7
Orthographic	645	144.9	29.5

Planned comparisons:
Control, Morphological: $t(23) = 5.25, p < .0001$
Control, Identical: $t(23) = 3.01, p = .006$
Control, Orthographic: $t(23) = 6.38, p < .0001$
Identical, Morphological: $t(23) = 2.61, p = .01$
Identical, Orthographic: $t(23) = 3.67, p = .001$
Morphological, Orthographic: $t(23) = -2.30, p = .02$

tween morphological and orthographic priming: the 96-millisecond advantage of the orthographic-priming condition over the identical-priming condition was significant ($t(23) = 3.67$, $p = .001$), as was the 33-millisecond advantage of the orthographic-priming condition over the morphological-priming condition ($t(23) = -2.30, p = .02$).

Conclusion

A different pattern of results was provoked in experiment 2 by using the same design and procedure as in experiment 1 but exchanging regular and irregular inflected French verbs for

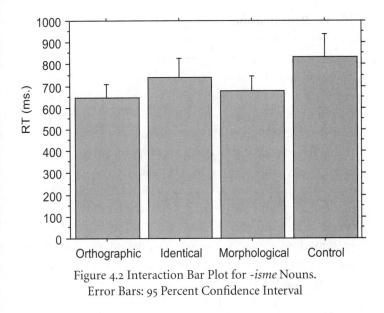

Figure 4.2 Interaction Bar Plot for *-isme* Nouns.
Error Bars: 95 Percent Confidence Interval

productively and unproductively suffixed French nouns. In experiment 1, with both regular and irregular French verbs it was possible to separate the effects of identical and morphological priming from priming between length- and frequency-matched controls and priming between form-related items. In experiment 2, with French nouns suffixed with *-isme* it was possible to statistically separate the effects of morphological priming from those of orthographic priming. However, with French nouns suffixed with *-té*, it was not possible to separate morphological from orthographic priming. Given the diachronic evidence (i.e., the dictionary and corpus data described earlier) arguing against the productive status of the *-té* suffix, my interpretation of this result is that participant responses in the morphological-priming condition were based not on derivational morphological relations between primes and stimuli, but on the form overlap shared by primes and stimuli in that condition.

This set of results suggests that French nouns suffixed with *-isme* and *-té* are represented differently in the French mental lexicon; while the separability of morphological priming from form priming points to *-isme* nouns' being the product of derivational rules, the inseparability of morphological priming from form priming indicates that *-té* nouns are stored as morphologically simple words that are retrieved whole from memory. I posited earlier that if this difference in representation were to be observed, it would constitute evidence in favor of words and rules theory as a viable theory of lexical representation in French. This is in fact the interpretation that I endorse. By providing a missing piece of supporting evidence, this finding is resonant with and lends strength to the conclusion of Meunier and Marslen-Wilson (2000) that a dual-mechanism theory of lexical representation is applicable in the case of French.

Thus far, evidence in favor of a dual-mechanism account of lexical representation has come from studies examining the processing of words. I will next consider evidence from another source, namely, studies of sentence-level processing, which will be used to shed light on a slightly different issue: the processing of derived nouns not as isolated words, but in the context of sentences.

V

Syntactic Priming
with French Nouns

The previous masked-priming experiments were designed to investigate the lexical representation of isolated French verbs and nouns. In line with earlier studies, findings from the study with French verbs suggested that both regular and irregular French verbs are processed using rules. The findings of the study with productively and unproductively suffixed French nouns were interpreted as providing evidence for words, that is, linguistic items that in words and rules theory are stored in and retrieved from a partly associative memory. The existence of such items had not been established in previous French studies.

In this chapter, I will again investigate the processing of nouns, though this time in the context of sentences. Many researchers hold that sentences such as *That's the man I saw crossing the street* contain silent, syntactically active traces of displaced nouns (i.e., *the man* in this example) at points in the sentence where they would occur by default (i.e., following the inflected verb *saw;* cf. *I saw the man crossing the street*). My motivation for switching from word-level priming to sentence-level priming is simple: I was keenly interested in seeing whether the behavioral patterns observed in my previous noun experiment with masked primes would surface in the context of sentences containing silent primes in the form of syntactic movement traces. If we were to observe similar priming at the sentence level, this would constitute evidence that words and rules theory holds not only at the word level, but also at the sentence level. Moreover, a result in line with the predictions of words and rules theory would also serve to further validate the *trace reactivation account* (Nicol and Swinney, 1989), a symbolically based theory of sentence processing. Thus, the sentence-level experiment described in this chapter served two related purposes: as a testing platform for words and rules theory at the sentence level, and as an attempt at further validation of the trace reactivation account.

Sentence-Level Studies

In standard analyses of sentence 5.1, the noun *professionalism* is the direct object of the transitive verb *showed.*

> **5.1** The shopkeeper admired the professionalism $_i$ which his employee showed $_i$ during the altercation with the customer.

In declarative English sentences, direct objects normally follow transitive verbs, yet in the above sentence *professionalism* actually precedes its verb. As a result, sentences such as 5.1 are said to contain gaps, that is, locations in a sentence where a sentential element should logically appear but in actual fact does not. Specifically, in sentence 5.1, the gap follows the verb *showed,* while the displaced gap filler is the noun *professionalism.* Such filler-gap constructions are of interest since speakers seem to process them effortlessly despite not being able to rely upon word order to do so.

Syntactic theories such as *principles and parameters* and frameworks such as *minimalism* (e.g., Chomsky, 1993; 1995) posit that when nouns appear in atypical locations—such as *professionalism* in sentence 5.1—they do not represent exceptional in situ constructions but instead instances of overt *operator* or *wh*-movement, that is, instances in which a noun phrase is generated in one location of a sentence but actually moves or is displaced to a different location in that sentence.[12] In sentence 5.1, the dependency, or relation, between the moved noun *professionalism* and its original location following the transitive verb *showed* is indicated by subscript *i*'s.

The Psychological Reality of Traces

What is of interest to the present discussion is that according to principles and parameters theory and minimalism, the movement of a noun (or a verb; see the following chapter for discussion) results in the creation of a silent, syntactically active copy, or trace, of the moved noun in its original location. But are traces psychologically real? That is, are speakers of a language measurably sensitive to this theoretical construct? In fact, there is evidence that traces of moved nouns do have psychological validity. Consider, for instance, the distribution of the English *wanna* (*want to*) construction (see, e.g., Lakoff, 1970). While for most native English speakers it should be possible to contract *want to* into *wanna* in sentence 5.2, use of *wanna* should be far less acceptable in sentence 5.3.

5.2 Which horse $_i$ do you want to / wanna win $_i$?

5.3 Which horse $_i$ do you want $_i$ to / *wanna win the race?

Sentence 5.2 should be understood as meaning *Which horse do you want to take possession of?* Sentence 5.3 should be understood as meaning *Which horse do you want to be victorious?* Given these glosses, for many speakers of English the *wanna* contraction is possible only with objects of infinitival complements. Thus in sentence 5.2, as indicated by the subscript *i*'s, there is a dependency between the noun phrase *which horse* and the position of object following the infinitive *to win*. By contrast, in sentence 5.3 *which horse* moved from the position of subject of the infinitive *to win*. The explanation offered for the distribution of *wanna* in the above sentences concerns the noun phrase *which horse* and the contrasting locations of the gap, or the empty slot in the sentence where *which horse* originally was. Ignoring a few details that are not relevant to the discussion, it is the presence of the gap (in different terms, the presence of the trace from *which horse*) between *want* and *to* that is said to block *wanna* contraction in sentence 5.3. As the gap, or trace, is not between *want* and *to* in sentence 5.2, contraction of *wanna* is possible.[13]

Intriguingly, there is behavioral evidence for the psychological reality of traces. This evidence comes primarily from studies investigating the processing of filler-gap constructions resembling those in sentences 5.1–5.3 through use of cross-modal lexical-decision tasks (this technique is described below; for additional details see Swinney et al., 1979; Tabossi, 1996). By and large, the results of these studies offer compelling evidence that syntactic traces do have psychological validity during on-line sentence processing.

Priming with Overt Anaphors at Trace Points

Nicol (1988; reported in Nicol and Swinney, 1989) had English native-speaking participants take part in a cross-modal lexical-decision task, which is so named because the task involves the presentation of primes and stimulus items through different modalities. This paradigm typically entails the use of auditory primes together with visual stimuli; the idea is that crossing modalities will encourage participants to respond using abstract (i.e., not modality-specific) language representations. In Nicol's study, participants listened to sentences that were similar to sentences 5.4a and 5.4b.

5.4a The boxer told the skier that the doctor for the team would blame himself for the injuries.

5.4b The boxer told the skier that the doctor for the team would blame him for the injuries.

Immediately following the words *himself* and *him* during sentence playback, participants were visually presented with letter strings corresponding to both real and nonce words. The real words included words that were semantically related to *boxer, skier,* and *doctor.* The participants' task was to make lexical decisions on the visually presented letter strings.

The sentences used by Nicol differed in that while sentence 5.4a contains the anaphor (i.e., reflexive or reciprocal pronoun) *himself,* sentence 5.4b contains the pronoun *him.* According to principles A and B of the *binding theory* (Chomsky, 1986), an anaphor must be bound within a local domain, which approximately means that an anaphor must have an antecedent within the clause that contains the anaphor, while pronouns must be free within a local domain (they must not have clause-internal antecedents). This means that in sentence 5.4a, the only possible antecedent for *himself* is *doctor*, since neither *boxer* nor *skier* belong to the same clause as the one that contains *doctor* and *himself*. By the same token, in sentence 5.4b, the only possible antecedents for the pronoun *him* are *boxer* and *skier*, since pronouns must not have clause-internal antecedents.

Analyses of reaction times to lexical decisions revealed that the predictions of the binding theory were in fact borne out: Nicol found that following the word *himself* in sentence 5.4a, priming effects were greater for *doctor* than for *boxer* and *skier*, while following *him* in sentence 5.4b, priming effects were greater for *boxer* and *skier* than for *doctor*. Nicol interpreted these results as evidence that the parser, or human language-processor, only considers syntactically available antecedents during coreference resolution.

Nicol (1988) also demonstrated that in sentences such as 5.5a and 5.5b below, priming effects similar to those reported with sentences 5.4a and 5.4b were only observed for antecedents with the appropriate number and gender.

> **5.5a** The boxer told the actress that the doctor for the team would blame her for the injuries.

> **5.5b** The boxers told the skier that the doctor for the team would blame them for the injuries.

Nicol found that in sentence 5.5a, there were priming effects for *actress* but not for *boxer* following *her*. In sentence

5.5b, Nicol observed priming effects for *boxers,* but not for *skier* following *them.* Such a result is in keeping with the hypothesis that traces contain both semantic and grammatical information related to their antecedents.

Priming with Covert Anaphors at Trace Points

In Swinney et al., 1988 (reported in Nicol and Swinney, 1989), participants listened to English relative-clause constructions containing gaps that themselves contained *wh*-traces. Sentence 5.6 below is an example of such a construction. As indicated by the subscripts, the noun phrase *the boy* is coreferenced with the empty trace in the gap following the verb *accused.* At three different moments during the temporal unfolding of the sentence, participants saw words that were either associated with or unrelated to the *wh*-moved noun. These visually presented probes appeared just before, at, and shortly after the syntactically defined *wh*-trace point (in sentence 5.6, these three points are indicated in brackets; the *t* represents the trace from *the boy*).

5.6 The policeman saw the boy $_i$ that the crowd at the party [pre- trace point] accused t_i [trace point] of the [post-trace point] crime.

Note that sentence 5.6 is different than the sentences in 5.4 and 5.5 in that while the previous sentences contained overt, or phonetically realized, anaphors (i.e., *himself, him, her,* and *them*), sentence 5.6 instead contains a covert, or phonetically null, anaphor immediately following the verb *accused.* Despite this difference, however, the results were similar to what had been observed with overt anaphors: Swinney et al. (1988)

found that lexical decisions to visual probes associated with
boy were significantly faster when they appeared at the trace
and post-trace points than when they appeared at the pre-trace
point.[14] By contrast, both lexical decisions and naming times
to visual probes associated with *crowd* and *policeman* failed to
show this pattern of results. From these findings, Swinney et al.
concluded that similar to overt anaphors, *wh*-traces prime
their antecedents.

The results of these studies and others like it (e.g., Nicol,
Fodor, and Swinney, 1994) have been interpreted as evidence
for the trace reactivation account. According to this account of
filler-gap processing, when the parser encounters what it rec-
ognizes as a displaced constituent (i.e., a filler), it retains the
constituent in memory until it encounters its associated gap.
At that time, the semantico-grammatical features of the displaced constituent are recalled from memory and regenerated
by the parser; this process then leads to the establishment of a
chain or dependency between the filler and gap, at which time
the phonetically null trace becomes syntactically active at the
gap site.

There is a possible single-mechanism alternative to the
symbolic trace reactivation account. Similar to connectionism, the *competition model* (e.g., Bates and MacWhinney, 1989;
MacWhinney and Bates, 1978;) also espouses a bottom-up,
data-driven perspective on language processing. In contrast to
connectionism, however, the competition model was designed
specifically to account for sentence processing. Further details
follow; however, it should become clear that owing to the design
and theoretical assumptions underlying the present sentence-
level studies, the competition model does not make clear predictions concerning the processing of sentences containing
wh-moved elements.

The Competition Model

According to MacWhinney (1997; in press; see also Bates and MacWhinney, 1989; MacWhinney and Bates, 1978; inter alia), the competition model is a functionalist, connectionist view of both first- and second-language acquisition that attributes linguistic development to learning and transfer. The model is functionalist in that forms of language are held to be determined and shaped by the communicative functions they serve. Moreover, in the competition model, language learning proceeds largely as a function of experience with a language. Thus the competition model contrasts with parameter-setting theories of language acquisition (cf. Chomsky, 1981; 1986; 1995) in that language form and function are seen as inseparable, and that language learning is largely a probabilistic, input-driven endeavor.

In the competition model, sentence comprehension and production processes are held to be the result of competition between cues, that is, competition between the various sources of information pertaining to linguistic form-function mappings. To take one example, the individual phones making up a word (i.e., a word's form) serve as cues to activating the meaning of that word from among the meanings of other similar words (e.g., the phones [ʃjɛ̃] serve as cues to activate the French word *chien*, "dog," rather than a word with a similar onset such as *chat*, "cat," [ʃa]). For production, required meanings or functions serve as cues for selecting an appropriate word from among different possible words.

As another example of competition between cues, languages that have a subject-verb-object (SVO) declarative word order will vary with respect to the extent to which they will use the cue of word order to encode semantic relations. Most competition model studies exploit this and other related cross-linguistic word-order differences to examine their relative contributions to sentence-level comprehension. In these studies, various cues are put into competition with one another, making it possible to estimate the strengths of particular cues for different languages. Successful sentence interpretation in these studies is defined as the ability to answer the question of who did what to whom. For instance, studies in this tradition have shown that while English and Italian are both SVO languages, they have rather different strengths for basic cues to sentence interpretation. In English, word order is the strongest cue to establishing agency (i.e., the doer of the action) in a sentence; thus, when a noun appears preverbally, this is interpreted as a very reliable cue to identifying the performer of the action of the sentence. Other possible cues such as agreement and animacy (i.e., being animate) are only important when there is no preverbal noun (i.e., in a verb-noun-noun sentence). In the case of Italian, however, studies have shown that agreement is a much stronger cue than word order (see, e.g., MacWhinney and Bates, 1978).

A crucial claim of the competition model is that cue strength in adult native speakers is directly proportional to *cue validity*, that is, the likelihood that some event will co-occur with a given cue. Studies have shown that in first language acquisition, children begin by orienting to the simplest or most available cues that indicate who did what to whom in a language (where simple and available roughly mean more frequent or phonologically salient). At later stages of acquisition, children gradually come to rely less upon a cue's availability and more upon its reliability, that is, the degree to which a cue can be trusted to indicate agency in the face of other, competing cues (this last concept has also been called *conflict validity*).

For example, in English the preverbal positioning cue for nouns is normally both available and (to a lesser degree) reliable. However, when the positioning cue is put into direct conflict with the case-marking cue, for instance, the third-person-singular personal pronouns *he/him* and *she/her,* the case marking cue will always win with older children and adults but not with younger children.

As mentioned above, competition model studies focus on comprehension strategies. Such studies typically involve participants listening to sequences of nouns and verbs (typically two nouns and one verb); for each sequence they hear, participants are asked to indicate on a scoring sheet which of the two nouns in the sequence was the doer of the action in the sequence. Participants are sometimes, though not always, encouraged to indicate their answers as quickly as possible. In designing the sequences, researchers fully cross variables such as noun animacy, case, word order, agreement, etc., such that the sequences will appear to be both grammatical (e.g., *the dog chases the cat*) and ungrammatical (e.g., *chases the dog the cat*).

In order to better illustrate the procedures according to which many of the aforementioned findings were obtained, I will now describe a study that is representative of how support for the model is typically found. In this study, Heilenman and McDonald (1993) had 135 participants: 15 monolingual French, 15 bilingual French-English, and 112 English first-language learners of French enrolled in first- to fourth-semester college-level French (henceforth, French L2 learners). The participants listened to seventy-two French word sequences, each of which contained two animate nouns (*la maman,* "mama," *le papa,* "papa," etc., from a list of twelve such nouns) and also one of three causative *faire* constructions, that is, constructions signifying that some agent is causing someone or something else to do something: *faire bouger,* "to make move," *faire tomber,* "to make fall," and *faire tourner,* "to make turn"). These noun-causative *faire*-noun sequences occurred in one of three word orders: noun-verb-noun (NVN), noun-noun-verb (NNV), and verb-noun-noun (VNN). The sequences also contained one of three combinations of clitic pronouns (subject only, e.g., *il* or *elle,* "he" or "she"; object only, e.g., *le* or *la,* "him" or "her"; and both subject and object clitics), as well as one of three kinds of clitic pronoun-noun gender agreement (agreement with both nouns, agreement indicating that the first noun was the subject, or agreement indicating that the second noun was the subject). A representative NVN sequence with a clitic subject pronoun agreeing with both nouns would be *la maman elle fait bouger la princesse,* "the mother she makes the princess move." These French sequences were presented to the bilingual French-English (control) and French L2 groups. A similar set of English materials was created and presented to an English native-speaker control group.

Analyses of the dependent measure, defined in this and other competition model studies as the percentage of responses in which a participant chooses the first noun as the doer of the action, revealed a complex set of findings. Briefly stated, the English native-speaker controls in the study tended to assign agency based upon word order, while the bilingual French-English controls tended to assign agency based upon clitic pronoun–noun gender agreement. Closer examination of the French L2 learners' interpretations of the French sequences indicated that in contrast to English native-speaker controls, the French L2 learners did not rely upon word order to assign agency, yet they did not use the same sequence interpretation strategies as the French native-speaker controls. Consistent French-native-like use of the clitic pronoun–noun gender-agreement cue did not surface, even among the fourth-semester French L2 learners. There was, however, evidence of restructuring and abandoning of inappropriate L1 (first language) cues in that the more advanced learners gradually adopted sequence interpretation strategies like French native-speakers.

The Competition Model and Trace Reactivation

As evidenced by its methods and its object of inquiry, the competition model seeks to explain sentence (or sequence) processing in probabilistic, functional terms. Put differently, the competition model does not seek to explain processing purely in structural or grammatical terms. This means that in contrast to the trace reactivation account, the competition model was not conceived as an account of syntactic processing in the context of the sentence-level cross-modal lexical-decision experiments reported above. Although it is likely the most extensively tested functionalist and probabilistically based model of sentence processing—and a model that moreover offers accounts both of the acquisition and end-state of sentence-processing strategies—the theoretical underpinnings of the competition model eschew constructs such as traces, subcategorizers, dependencies, or (re)activation. Since the present studies take as a given the existence of these constructs, and since the trace reactivation account cannot truthfully be described as functionalist, direct comparisons of the two models appear to be impossible. Strictly speaking, therefore, the competition model would appear to have little to say regarding the processing implications of the theoretical constructs presently under investigation.

This is not to say that in a more general sense, a data-driven account of sentence processing would make no predictions concerning the results of a sentence-level cross-modal lexical-decision experiment. On the contrary, one could say that to the extent to which relative-clause sentences such as *The boss admired the dynamism that his employees showed at yesterday's meeting* and declarative SVO sentences such as *The boss's employees showed dynamism at yesterday's meeting* are licensed by a grammar, as they are in English and in French, a data-driven theory of sentence processing could account for faster lexical decisions to *dynamism* following the verb *showed* in the relative-clause sentence by claiming that participants were simply responding according to statistical regularities in the language. That is, given that sentences in a language are more frequently SVO than OVS, and that speakers of a language can become "tuned" to this and other statistical regularities in the syntax of a language, speakers of a language could come to expect that all things being equal, linguistic items will tend to follow one another in particular temporal orders. In the context of a cross-modal lexical-decision experiment that includes sentences such as *The boss admired the dynamism that his employees showed at yesterday's meeting,* faster lexical decisions to visually presented *dynamism* following the auditory offset of *showed* would by such thinking have no basis in syntactic theory but would instead be the result of a participant's experience that very often a noun object will follow its verb.

I do not wish to deny the utility of appealing to a probabilistic, data-driven perspective for addressing questions concerning language processing. I simply hold that for the present studies it is pointless to do so. A consequence of the built-in assumptions and design of the present experiments is that while they will allow for the falsification of a symbolic account, they will not allow for the falsification of a data-driven perspective. That is, a general data-driven account of sentence processing could not be confirmed or disconfirmed either by finding evidence of priming at trace points or by not finding such evidence. For this reason, I will not give further attention either to the competition model or to more general data-driven accounts of sentence processing and will instead focus on symbolic accounts.

Later, we will see that there is a viable symbolic alternative interpretation of the data cited in support of the trace reactivation account. That alternative interpretation is itself based upon a different theory of sentence processing, the *direct association hypothesis* (Pickering and Barry, 1991). The competing predictions of the two theories serve as the motivation for a final experiment, the results of which offer a way of distinguishing between the two theories. For now, however, we will begin by describing an experiment based upon the theory just outlined (the trace reactivation account).

Experiment 3: Syntactic Priming of French Nouns

This experiment was designed to investigate whether French nouns can be primed by the syntactic structure of the utterances in which they appear. Of particular interest in this study is the interaction between knowledge of noun movement (specifically, *wh*-traces) and knowledge of noun morphology. The amount of syntactic priming was compared between more-productive and less-productive derivationally suffixed nouns and their base forms, and between word and nonword control conditions.

The experiment in this chapter was designed to provide a perspective on the relative contributions of syntactic and morphological knowledge to online processing. The basic design of the experiment is similar to that used by Swinney et al.

(1988), though here as elsewhere in this book, the participants and the language tested will be French not English. Auditory primes consisted of French sentences containing *wh*-moved elements. Visually presented targets appeared at three different points during the playback of a carrier sentence: before the location of a trace point, at the location of a trace point, and after the location of a trace point.

Swinney et al. used targets that were semantically related to moved elements. Recall now the results of the earlier experiment with French nouns:

1. Derived *té*-suffixed French nouns (e.g., *propreté*) are not productive, and hence they are not decomposed into their component parts by French speakers. That is, derived *té*-suffixed French nouns represent frozen forms that, for processing purposes, are treated by French speakers as whole, idiosyncratic word-chunks.

2. Derived *isme*-suffixed French nouns (e.g., *capital-isme*) are productive, and they are automatically decomposed into their component parts (e.g., *capital* and *-isme*) by French speakers. Put differently, derived *isme*-suffixed French nouns are the product of a suffixation rule that French speakers use to produce and understand such words.

For the present experiment, the visually presented targets for the *wh*-moved elements will be changed from semantically related words to morphologically related ones, specifically to productively derived *-isme* nouns and unproductively derived *-té* nouns. Assuming that *wh*-movement is a form of symbolic computation, and assuming that words and rules theory is applicable to sentence-level processing the way it has been shown to be for word level processing, this should result in a measurable interaction between syntax and morphological productivity.

METHOD
Participants

Twenty-eight native speakers of French (mean age 29; range 24–42) with normal or corrected vision participated in this experiment. Subjects were recruited in France and from communities surrounding the University of Oregon in Eugene, Oregon, and the University of Illinois at Urbana-Champaign.

Stimuli

Fifty test sentences (twenty-five containing moved *isme*-suffixed nouns, and twenty-five containing moved *té*-suffixed nouns) were created for this experiment (see the appendix for the complete list of sentences). All were declaratives with tensed, transitive main verbs and *wh*-moved nouns originating from within object relative clauses, such as in sentence 5.7 (sentence 5.7a is a translation).

> **5.7** *Le juge n'a pas pardonné le barbarisme $_i$ que la foule sur la place a montré t $_i$ pendant la manifestation.*

> **5.7a** The judge did not pardon the barbarism $_i$ that the crowd in the square showed t $_i$ during the demonstration.

The sentences contained an average of 18.2 words each (range approximately 16–23 words). A female French native speaker was digitally recorded (sampling rate 22050 Hz; 16 bit quantization; in stereo) while reading the sentences at a normal rate of speaking. The average duration of the test sentences was 5.4 seconds. Using a sound editor, cursors were placed into the resulting sound files at three different locations: immediately preceding the tensed verb within the relative clause, immediately following the tensed verb within the relative clause (this corresponded to the trace position), and between the determiner and the noun within the sentence-final noun phrase. These cursors served as prompts for displaying one of four types of visual targets during the audio playback of a sentence: identical targets (e.g., *barbarisme*), morphologically related targets (e.g., *barbare*), frequency- or length-matched control targets (e.g., *chevelures*), and nonce targets (e.g., **bicron*). The resulting design included twenty-five test sentences, times four types of visual targets, times three points of target appearance, for a total of three hundred trials, of which seventy-five were nonce-word trials. To have an equal number of real- and nonce-word trials, an additional fifty "distracter" sentences were created. These were similar in structure to the test items but with only nonce-word targets appearing at three different places during audio playback, for a total of 150 additional nonce-word trials. The final number of trials included 225 real-word trials, and 225 nonce-word trials, for a total of 450 trials. In order to prevent subjects from being presented with the same sentence twice, items were counterbalanced across experimental lists according to visual-target type, visual-target position, and syntactic-priming condition. In order to have a baseline condition from which to measure effects of syntactic priming, a separate set of items was created from the items containing instances of *wh-* movement. Each of the original test sentences also contained a noun that had not undergone movement (e.g., *foule*, from sentence 5.7 above). In the baseline condition, visually presented targets were based on these nouns rather than on the *wh*-moved nouns. For this second set of items, the same three syntactically defined cursor points (pre-trace, trace, and post-trace) were used to display one of three kinds of visual targets: an identical target (e.g., *foule*), a frequency- or length-matched control target (e.g., *micro*), and a nonce target (e.g., **bicron*).[15] The resulting design contained twenty-five test sentences, times three types of visual targets, times three points of target appearance, for a total of 225 trials, of which seventy-five were nonce-word trials. To balance the number of word and nonword trials, an additional twenty-five distracter sentences were created. These were similar in structure to the test items but with only nonce-word targets appearing at three different places during audio playback, for a total of seventy-five nonceword trials. The final number of trials in the baseline syntactic-priming set included 150 real-word trials and 150 nonceword trials, for a total of 300 trials. In order to prevent subjects from being presented with the same sentence twice, items were counterbalanced across experimental lists (ten baseline, eleven critical, for a total of twenty-one lists) according to visual-target type, visual-target position, and syntactic-priming condition. Fifteen participants were tested on the critical sentences, while the remaining thirteen were tested on the baseline sentences.[16]

PROCEDURE

Subjects were tested individually in a quiet room. Written instructions specified that subjects were to listen to short French sentences playing over their headphones, and that at different moments during a sentence's playback, a string of letters would appear at the center of their computer screen (marked with two crosses: ++). The instructions specified that while some letter strings would be legitimate French words (e.g., *chien*), others would not be (e.g., **crien*), and that upon the appearance of each string the subject was to decide as quickly as possible whether it constituted a legitimate French word. The instructions emphasized both speed and accuracy in responding.

Trials began with a five-hundred-millisecond pause, followed by the display of a focus point at the center of the computer screen (++). Following another five-hundred-millisecond pause, a sentence began playing over the subject's headphones. When a cursor was reached in a given sound file, the focus point was replaced by a target word, which appeared on-screen for one second or until the subject pressed a response button.

PREDICTIONS: PRODUCTIVELY SUFFIXED -*ISME* NOUNS WITH *WH*-MOVEMENT SENTENCES

Sentence 5.8 is an example of the auditorially presented French sentences in which the -*isme* noun (i.e., *professionalisme*) has undergone *wh*- movement, presumably leaving behind a phonetically empty, syntactically active trace in its original location.

> **5.8** *Le commerçant a admiré le professionalisme $_i$ que son employé* [pre-trace point] *a montré t $_i$* [trace point] *pendant l'altercation avec* [post-trace point] *le client.*

> **5.8a** The shopkeeper admired the professionalism $_i$ which his employee [pre-trace point] showed *t $_i$* [trace point] during the altercation with [post-trace point] the customer.

If *wh*-movement is in fact best described in terms of symbolic rules that have psychological reality, then compared to frequency- and length-matched control words, there should be a priming advantage in the form of faster lexical decisions for identical visual stimuli at the trace point, and possibly at the post-trace point; this priming advantage should not obtain, or at least be less robust, at the pre-trace point. Furthermore, if the phonetically empty traces in the auditorily presented sentences are both syntactically and lexically active, then with *isme*-suffixed nouns there should be an equally strong priming advantage for morphologically related targets at the points where such priming is observed with identical targets. These findings should obtain in spite of the fact that, temporally speaking, the pre-trace point in the auditory sentence is closer to the actual utterance of the displaced *wh*-word than is the trace point.

PREDICTIONS: UNPRODUCTIVELY SUFFIXED -*TÉ* NOUNS WITH *WH*-MOVEMENT SENTENCES

Sentence 5.9 is an example of the auditorially presented French sentences in which the noun (*saleté,* "mess") has undergone *wh*-movement, presumably leaving behind a phonetically empty, syntactically active trace in its original location.

5.9 *Le patron n'a pas apprécie la saleté $_i$ que les invités du mariage* [pre-trace point] *ont laissée t $_i$* [trace point] *dans la salle de* [post-trace point] *séjour.*

5.9a The boss did not appreciate the mess $_i$ that the wedding guests [pre-trace point] left t_i [trace point] in the living [post-trace point] room.

Again, through priming from inaudible, syntactically active (and psychologically real) traces, French speakers should
show a priming advantage (in the form of faster lexical decisions) for identical targets at the trace point; this priming advantage should not obtain, or at least be less robust, at the
pre-trace point. These findings should obtain even though,
temporally speaking, the pre-trace point in the auditory sentence is closer to the actual utterance of the displaced *wh*-word
than is the trace point.

However, the *-té* suffix is not productive like the *-isme*
suffix. Therefore, at the trace point, relative to frequency- and
length-matched controls, there should be a significant priming advantage for identical targets, but there should be no such
advantage for morphologically related targets. Such a finding
is expected since in contrast to productively suffixed *-isme*
nouns, *té*-suffixed French nouns represent frozen, nondecomposable forms. Therefore, while identical targets such as *saleté*
should prompt faster lexical decisions than controls at trace
points, there should be no such advantage for morphologically
related targets such as *sale* since French speakers should not
automatically decompose the silent, syntactically active trace
of *saleté* into its component parts upon encountering it at the
trace point.

PREDICTIONS: BASELINE SENTENCES

In contrast to targets related in some way to *wh*-moved nouns,
there should be no reactivation of any baseline nouns (i.e.,
nouns that have not undergone *wh*-movement) at any of the
trace points. Any evidence of reactivation with baseline nouns
would cast serious doubt upon the trace reactivation account.

RESULTS

RTs greater than 1,500 milliseconds were discarded. This resulted in a loss of 2.7 percent of the data. Errors, which constituted less than 2 percent of the data and which occurred exclusively with critical items and marginally more frequently with *té*-suffixed nouns, were also removed from the data prior to analysis. As in the previous experiment, to reduce skew while retaining numerical outliers, RTs were inversely transformed prior to statistical analysis. ANOVAs examining the factor of list for critical and baseline sentences revealed that there was no effect of list for either set of sentences; therefore, results from all lists were combined.

For these and the other results presented below, the degree of priming and evidence of trace reactivation were determined as follows. For each point during the auditory playback of a sentence at which a target was visually presented (i.e., at pre-trace, trace, and post-trace points), an ANOVA was run on the RTs to identical, morphologically related, and control targets that were presented at that point. Significant priming was claimed in cases where for a given point, there were significant differences between RTs to identical versus control targets or between RTs to morphological versus control targets. Evidence of trace reactivation was claimed when there was significant priming at a point predicted to contain a silent, syntactically active trace by the trace reactivation account.

Findings: Unproductively Suffixed -té Nouns with wh-Movement Sentences

For reference, sentence 5.9 above is repeated here as sentence 5.10.

5.10 *Le patron n'a pas apprécie la saleté $_i$ que les invités du mariage* [pre-trace point] *ont laissée t $_i$* [trace point] *dans la salle de* [post-trace point] *séjour.*

Table 5.1 charts the mean RTs by target type (identical, morphologically related, and control) for *té*-suffixed nouns at the pre-trace point. The ANOVA run on these RTs revealed that there were significant differences in RT (F (2, 13) = 4.8, p = .01). Planned comparisons revealed significant differences between control targets and identical targets, and between control targets and morphologically related targets (t (13) = 2.2, p = .04, and t (13) = 3.3, p = .005, respectively).[17]

Table 5.2 charts the mean RTs by target type (identical,

Table 5.1. Means table for RTs to *té*-suffixed nouns; pre-trace point

	Count	Mean RT	Std. Dev.	Std. Err.
Control	14	847	235.6	62.9
Identical	14	774	178.5	47.7
Morphological	14	770	212.2	56.7

Table 5.2. Means table for RTs to *té*-suffixed nouns; trace point

	Count	Mean RT	Std. Dev.	Std. Err.
Control	15	869	273	70.5
Identical	15	794	200.8	51.8
Morphological	15	860	252.7	65.2

Table 5.3. Means table for RTs to *té*-suffixed nouns; post-trace point

	Count	Mean RT	Std. Dev.	Std. Err.
Control	13	819	188.1	52.1
Identical	13	765	216.5	60
Morphological	13	869	215.2	59.6

morphologically related, and control) for *té*-suffixed nouns at the trace point. The ANOVA run on these RTs revealed no significant differences in RTs to targets ($F(2, 14) = .8$, $p = .4$).

Table 5.3 charts the mean RTs by target type (identical, morphologically related, and control) for *té*-suffixed nouns at the post-trace point. The ANOVA run on these RTs again revealed no significant differences in RTs to targets ($F(2, 12) = .9$, $p = .3$).

Results with *té*-suffixed nouns are summarized in table 5.4. From this presentation of the results, we can see that there is significant priming at the pre-trace point for both identical and morphologically related targets.[18] What is of more interest is that numerically speaking, there is some evidence of a pattern of activation at the trace point with identical targets, in that there is a seventy-three-millisecond RT advantage for identical targets versus control targets. However, the RT advantage is not statistically significant; it is also only half the magnitude of the statistically significant trace-point reactivation associated with *isme*-suffixed words (see table 5.8). This means that by my definition, and seemingly counter to the predictions of the trace reactivation account, there was no reactivation with *té*-suffixed nouns at the trace point for identical targets. Finally, there were no priming effects at the post-trace point.

Table 5.4. Priming advantage (lexical-decision RTs to control words minus RTs to test words, in milliseconds) for identical and morphologically related targets at each visual probe point; all -_té_ words

	Visual probe point		
	Pre-trace	Trace	Post-trace
Identical targets	73*	75	54
Morphologically related targets	77*	9	50

* $p < .05$

Findings: Productively Suffixed -isme Nouns with wh-Movement Sentences

We turn next to the results with _isme_-suffixed nouns. Again for reference, sentence 5.8 is repeated here as sentence 5.11.

5.11 _Le commerçant a admiré le professionalisme_ $_i$ _que son employé_ [pre-trace point] _a montré t_ $_i$ [trace point] _pendant l'altercation avec_ [post-trace point] _le client._

Table 5.5 charts the mean RTs by target type (identical, morphologically related, and control) for _isme_-suffixed nouns at the pre-trace point. The ANOVA run on these RTs revealed that there were significant differences in RT (F (2, 13) = 3.5, p = .04). Planned comparisons failed to find a significant difference between control targets and identical targets (p = .5), but they did reveal a significant difference between control targets and morphologically related targets (t (13) = 2.35, p = .03).

Table 5.6 charts the mean RTs by target type (identical,

Table 5.5. Means table for *isme*-suffixed nouns; pre-trace point

	Count	Mean RT	Std. Dev.	Std. Err.
Control	14	864	202.4	54.1
Identical	14	838	260.5	69.6
Morphological	14	760	230	61.4

morphologically related, and control) for *isme*-suffixed nouns at the trace point. The ANOVA run on these RTs revealed significant differences in RTs to targets ($F(2,13) = 14.9, p < .0001$). Planned comparisons revealed significant differences between control targets and identical targets, and between control targets and morphologically related targets ($t(13) = 5.3, p = .0001$, and $t(13) = 4.006, p = .001$, respectively). Additionally, a paired t test revealed that the difference between RTs to identical and morphologically related targets at the trace point was not significant ($t(13) = .6, p = .5$).

Table 5.7 charts the mean RTs by target type (identical, morphologically related, and control) for *isme*-suffixed nouns at the post-trace point. The ANOVA run on these RTs again revealed no significant differences in RTs to targets ($F(2,14) = .7, p = .4$).

Table 5.6. Means table for *isme*-suffixed nouns; trace point

	Count	Mean RT	Std. Dev.	Std. Err.
Control	14	898	217.2	58
Identical	14	754	207.5	55.46
Morphological	14	740	166.1	44.4

**Table 5.7. Means table for *isme*-suffixed nouns;
post-trace point**

	Count	Mean RT	Std. Dev.	Std. Err.
Control	15	840	197.6	51
Identical	15	842	285	73.5
Morphological	15	786	237.1	61.2

The results with *isme*-suffixed nouns are summarized in table 5.8. From this presentation of the results, we can see that there is significant priming at the pre-trace point for morphologically related targets. There is also evidence of trace reactivation with both identical and morphologically related targets, in that there is significant priming at the trace point: the 144-millisecond RT advantage for identical targets versus control targets is significant, as is the 158-millisecond RT advantage for morphologically related targets versus control targets. This means that by my definition and in accordance with the predictions of the trace reactivation account, there was reactivation at the trace point for identical targets. Moreover, supporting the claim that productively suffixed *-isme* nouns are rule generated, there was also reactivation at the trace point for morphologically related targets. Finally, there were no priming effects at the post-trace point.

Findings: Baseline (Non-wh-Movement) Sentences
Finally, we turn to the results with the baseline sentences. For reference, sentence 5.7 is repeated as sentence 5.12.

5.12 *Le juge n'a pas pardonné le barbarisme $_i$ que la foule sur la place a montré t $_i$ pendant la manifestation.*

Table 5.8 Priming advantage (lexical-decision RTs to control words minus RTs to test words, in milliseconds) for identical and morphologically related targets at each visual probe point; all *-isme* words

	Visual probe point		
	Pre-trace	Trace	Post-trace
Identical targets	26	144**	−2
Morphologically related targets	104*	158**	54

* $p < .05$

** $p < .01$

Recall that in the baseline sentences, non-*wh*-moved nouns such as *foule* were visually presented at the same three points (pre-trace, trace, and post-trace) as in the test sentences. On the assumption that the trace reactivation account is correct, no reactivation of non-*wh*-moved nouns was anticipated. This was in fact the result observed: there were no priming effects, and thus no evidence of trace reactivation, for non-*wh*-moved nouns at any of the three points tested in sentences containing *té-* and *isme*-suffixed nouns. Table 5.9 includes the ANOVAs and means tables for all the baseline conditions.

Conclusion

Together with the negative results of the baseline condition sentences, comparison of table 5.4 with table 5.8 suggests that changes in the productivity of the suffix of the *wh*-moved nouns resulted in changes in patterns of priming and trace reactivation. In particular, changes in patterns of trace reactiva-

Table 5.9. Results with baseline sentences from Experiment 3.

	Count	Mean RT	Std. Dev.	Std. Err.
ANOVA and means table for *té*-suffixed words; baseline sentences, pre-trace position: $F(1, 12) = 1.3, p = .27$				
Control	13	760	147.8	41.03
No movement	13	795	172.6	47.8
ANOVA and means table for *té*-suffixed words; baseline sentences, trace position: $F(1, 12) = 3.3, p = .09$				
Control	13	745	106.5	29.5
No movement	13	720	92.6	25.7
ANOVA and means table for *té*-suffixed words; baseline sentences, post-trace position: $F(1, 12) = 2.7, p = .12$				
Control	13	776	74.7	20.7
No movement	13	720	149.8	39.6
ANOVA and means table for *isme*-suffixed words; baseline sentences, pre-trace position: $F(1, 12) = 0.01, p = .9$				
Control	13	756	159.1	44.1
No movement	13	754	146.3	40.5

	Count	Mean RT	Std. Dev.	Std. Err.
ANOVA and means table for *isme*-suffixed words; baseline sentences, trace position: $F(1, 12) = 2.6, p = .12$				
Control	13	757	122.1	33.8
No movement	13	700	93.3	25.8
ANOVA and means table for *isme*-suffixed words; baseline sentences, post-trace position: $F(1, 12) = 1.3, p = .27$				
Control	13	714	95	26.3
No movement	13	689	102.5	28.4

tion, that is, priming at the trace point, largely support both the trace reactivation account and words and rules theory in that with *isme*-suffixed nouns, there was a statistically significant RT advantage at the trace point for both identical and morphologically related targets versus control targets. Although with *isme*-suffixed nouns there was also priming with morphologically related targets at the pre-trace point, the observed priming advantages are numerically greater at the trace point than at the pre-trace point for both identical and morphologically related targets. Temporally speaking, the trace point is further from the surface position of the displaced noun than is the pre-trace point; this suggests that pre-trace-point priming may represent a form of cross-modal, auditory-visual repetition priming. In contrast, the different pattern and magnitude of trace-point priming suggest that its source is not a form of cross-modal repetition priming. My view is that instead, it reflects priming from a silent, syntactically active trace of a displaced element related to an *isme*-suffixed French noun.

Recall, however, that while a numerical RT advantage was observed at the trace point for identical *té*-suffixed targets versus control targets, that numerical advantage was not statistically significant (in fact, there was not even evidence of a statistical trend toward a priming effect). At first glance, this is a surprising result in that even if no priming was anticipated for morphologically related targets, there was reason to expect trace reactivation for identical *té*-suffixed targets. Putting aside its surprising nature, and accepting it at face value, what does this result suggest with respect to the trace reactivation account? Taken together with the findings of the *isme*-suffixed nouns in our sentence-level study, and with the findings of our previous word-level experiments, this result suggests that in the case of *wh*-moved derived nouns, in order for priming to occur at trace positions with identical stimuli, the antecedent of the trace should be morphologically decomposable, that is, the *wh*-moved noun should bear a productive suffix.

The implications of the results with *té*-suffixed nouns also largely support the sentence-level applicability of words and rules theory. The finding that there was no reactivation of morphologically related targets with *té*-suffixed nouns was expected, as these represented unproductively suffixed, frozen forms.

In the following chapter, I will again consider the relationship between productive suffixation and identical priming in the context of sentence processing. I will also address the different predictions of the trace reactivation account and the direct association hypothesis. Doing so will call for a return to studying the processing of verbs, this time in a sentential context.

VI

Syntactic Priming with French Verbs

Using productively and unproductively derived French nouns and French participants, the experiment in the previous chapter was designed to test predictions of words and rules theory in the context of sentence processing. The experiment was also designed to further examine the efficacy of the trace reactivation account.

As we saw, the predictions of words and rules theory for sentence-level processing were largely borne out in that with *isme*-suffixed nouns, priming was observed between both identical and morphologically related targets and a hypothesized trace point, while with *té*-suffixed nouns, no priming was observed between morphologically related targets and a hypothesized trace point. However, seemingly counter to the expectations of the trace reactivation account, with *té*-suffixed nouns no priming was observed between identical targets and a hypothesized trace point. This result led me to conclude that in order for trace reactivation to occur with identical stimuli, the trace itself had to be coreferenced with a displaced item that bore a productive suffix.

In this chapter, I will outline an experiment that was partially motivated by this last finding. Like the previous experiment, the present study concerns a sentence-level cross-modal lexical-decision task in which primes are silent, syntactically active traces. In contrast to the previous study, however, traces in the present study will be coreferential not with productively and unproductively derived *wh*-moved nouns, but with inflected regular and irregular French verbs. Recall that distributional and experimental evidence suggests that inflections on both regular and irregular French verbs are both highly regular and productive. If it is the case that in order for trace reactivation to occur with identical primes, traces have to be coreferenced with a displaced item that bears a productive suffix, and assuming that trace reactivation occurs in a similar manner irrespective of the type of antecedent suffixation (i.e., inflectional or derivational), then in a sentence-level study using inflected regular and irregular French verbs, we should observe priming with both kinds of items.

Later, we will present a syntactic feature that, in the case of French, offers the possibility of testing for trace reactivation with displaced verbs. For now, however, we return to the question raised in the last chapter concerning the efficacy of the trace reactivation account. Recall that in the trace reactivation account of filler-gap processing, when the parser encounters a filler, it retains the filler in memory until it encounters the filler's associated gap. At that time, the parser recalls from memory and regenerates the semantico-grammatical features of the displaced constituent, leading to the establishment of a "chain," or dependency, between the filler and gap and resulting in the syntactically active status of the phonetically null trace at the gap site. Evidence in support of the trace reactivation account comes from studies conducted with English (Nicol, 1988; Nicol and Swinney, 1989; Nicol, Fodor, and Swinney, 1994) and with French (cf. the results of our previous sentence-level study with *wh*-moved French nouns). As alluded to in the last chapter, however, an alternative exists to the trace reactivation account in which neither movement nor trace reactivation play roles. This alternative account is presented below.

The Direct Association Hypothesis

The direct association hypothesis (Pickering and Barry, 1991) is a psycholinguistic account of the cross-modal lexical-decision data outlined above that relies neither upon gaps nor upon traces. Essentially, where the trace reactivation account posits a two-step procedure for processing filler-gap constructions (i.e., recall of a filler from memory and establishment of a dependency between filler and gap that results in trace creation at the gap site), the direct association hypothesis instead posits a single-step procedure according to which parsing a verb results in a direct (and immediate) association of the verb with the verb's arguments (i.e., its dependencies). This single-step procedure is schematized in sentence 6.1.

> **6.1** The policeman saw the boy $_i$ that the crowd at the party accused $_i$ of the crime.

According to the direct association hypothesis, when a person listening to sentence 6.1 reaches the verb *accused,* the verb's dependencies are directly associated with it. There is no need for the parser to wait for the gap following the verb *accused,* nor is there any need for the parser to establish a filler-gap dependency and create a trace at the gap site. Since most of the data supporting the trace reactivation account come from sentences such as 6.1, which feature transitive verbs, and given that in English, direct objects tend to follow their verbs, the direct association hypothesis holds that studies that appear to support the trace reactivation account have not taken into account the virtual overlap between canonical direct-object locations, which tend to follow the verb that subcategorizes them, and gap sites. In terms of the direct association hypothesis, only subcategorization facts (i.e., facts pertaining to any dependents of a verb or other subcategorizer) are of processing relevance; gaps and traces are epiphenomenal and irrelevant to processing.

The obvious question to ask is whether the trace reactivation account or the direct association hypothesis is the more veridical processing account. As we have seen, these two accounts differ in their interpretation of the results of the English filler-gap studies: while the trace reactivation account holds that antecedent priming effects at *wh*-trace gaps are owing to reactivation of the trace's syntactic and semantic features at the gap site, the direct association hypothesis maintains that antecedent priming effects at *wh*-trace gaps are the result of an association between the displaced constituent and the verb that subcategorizes it. Differently stated, in the trace reactivation account it is the trace that plays a crucial role in processing, while in the direct association hypothesis it is the association of the verb (or any subcategorizer) with its dependents that is key in processing.

Researchers have attempted to design sentences that would allow for a direct comparison between the trace reactivation account and the direct association hypothesis. Sentences such as 6.2, used by Nicol (1993), resolved the confound in sentences from previous studies between the gap site and the canonical direct-object location.

6.2 To which butcher did the woman who had just inherited a large sum of money give the very expensive gift the other day?

Nicol (1993) tested for antecedent priming of the prepositional phrase *to which butcher* following the verb *give* (i.e., in object position following the verb, where antecedent priming is predicted only by the direct association hypothesis) and following the noun *gift* (i.e., where the noun's prepositional phrase complement is thought to have originated from, and where antecedent priming is predicted only by the trace reactivation account). Results were inconclusive, however, in that antecedent priming was observed at both locations. In a further experiment with relative clause sentences such as 6.3, Nicol (1993) observed reactivation of a verb's subject following the verb *is*.

6.3 The actress who had caused such a sensation among the critics is a failure with the general public.

While this result is in keeping with the direct association hypothesis, the differences between sentences 6.1 and 6.2 and sentence 6.3 (e.g., use of transitive verbs vs. use of the verb *to be* and testing for reactivation of relativized objects vs. reactivation of relativized subjects, etc.) suggest that some caution should be exercised in making direct comparisons between the Nicol (1993) study and the other studies previously outlined.

There have also been studies that have examined the processing of languages such as German and Japanese, which owing to "object scrambling" can have traces that actually precede their verbs (for German, see, e.g., Clahsen and Featherston, 1999; for Japanese, see Nakano, Felser, and Clahsen, 2002). These languages thus offer the possibility of disentangling gap sites from verbs and other subcategorizers. By and large, these studies have found support for the trace reactivation account in that they have reported antecedent priming effects at gap sites that preceded (and therefore were not contiguous with) postverbal canonical object locations.

The Present Sentence-Level Study

In the experiment that follows, I aim to contribute in a different way to the trace reactivation account–direct association hypothesis debate. To date, studies have tested for reactivation of nouns; to the best of my knowledge, no one has tested for reactivation of *verbs*. Yet according to recent generative syntactic accounts (e.g., Pollock, 1989), French differs from English in a way that we may be able to exploit in order to shed further light upon the debate. Specifically, French differs from English in that it is a language with obligatory finite (i.e., tensed) lexical (as opposed to auxiliary) verb raising. It is finite lexical verb raising that allows for the left-to-right, verb-adverb order in French sentences such as 6.4 below.

6.4 *Jeannot fume souvent des cigarettes.*

The literal translation of this sentence, "Johnny smokes often cigarettes," contains a verb-adverb order that, to say the least, is strongly dispreferred in English (and while *Jeannot souvent fume des cigarettes* would likely be understood, the English word order of adverb-finite lexical verb is rather odd sounding in French). Further details will be provided below; for now, I will simply say that accounts in the syntactic literature suggest that in French, finite lexical verbs undergo obligatory movement (specifically, raising), and that this verb movement results in the creation of a trace in the verb's original location. This means that originally, the verb *fume* was generated to the right of the adverb before it raised to its surface location to the left of the adverb, presumably leaving a silent, syntactically active trace to the right of *souvent*. This is schematized in sentence 6.5.

6.5 *Jeannot fume*$_i$ *souvent t*$_i$ *des cigarettes.*

PREDICTIONS

On the assumption that traces are of processing relevance, and on the more speculative assumption that the parser will reconstitute traces similarly whether they result from displaced nouns or displaced verbs (and that therefore antecedent priming effects will arise at a trace point irrespective of the grammatical category of the displaced item), the trace reactivation account appears to make the following prediction regarding the processing of the hypothesized trace in sentence 6.5:

1. In a cross-modal lexical-decision experiment with auditorily presented French sentences containing finite lexical verbs that are thought to have obligatorily raised to the left of an adverb, and visually

presented letter strings representing raised verbs, the trace reactivation account predicts that there should be priming in the form of faster lexical decisions to raised verbs at the hypothesized trace point than at other points in the sentence.

By contrast, since the direct association hypothesis assumes that subcategorizers such as verbs are of processing relevance while gaps and traces are irrelevant to processing, a finding that supported the prediction above would have the following implication for the direct association hypothesis:

2. Given the same experimental paradigm, sentences, and stimuli, evidence of priming at the hypothesized trace point would be evidence against the direct association hypothesis.

This experiment will involve both identical primes, that is, finite lexical verbs, and morphologically related primes, that is, infinitival verb forms. If the findings of the word-level experiments with French verbs reported here and in Meunier and Marslen-Wilson, 2000—findings that were interpreted as supporting (or in our case, partially supporting) a dual-mechanism model of lexical representation—can be extended to sentence processing, then with auditory primes such as sentence 6.5 and with stimuli such as *fume* and *fumer* ("he/she smokes" and "to smoke," respectively), we should observe the following:

3. Given the same experimental paradigm, sentences, and stimuli, a dual-mechanism model such as words and rules theory predicts that priming should be observed with both regular and irregular French verbs when the visual stimulus at the

trace point is either the raised verb itself or the verb's root form.

A final prediction can be made with respect to the finding from the sentence-level study with French nouns, which seemed to suggest that trace reactivation with identical primes occurred only in cases where the item in question was morphologically decomposable. This leads to the following prediction:

4. Given the same experimental paradigm, sentences, and stimuli, trace reactivation with identical primes should be observed with both regular and irregular French verbs.

LIMITATIONS

With respect to the predictions made above, some caution will be in order in interpreting the findings of our sentence-level verb study. To my knowledge, there are no data that address real-time processing questions concerning raised verbs, either in English or in any other language. This means that we know very little concerning the extent to which existing analyses of French lexical verb raising have measurable behavioral consequences. For instance, it may be the case that for independent reasons, different trace-related phenomena are handled differently by the parser and therefore have very different behavioral consequences, some of which may be poorly captured (if at all) using measures such as reaction times to cross-modal primed lexical decisions. Also, even casual comparison of the English sentences containing relative clauses and covert anaphors such as 5.8 and 5.9 from the previous chapter with declarative French sentences containing raised lexical verbs such as 6.5 above reveals some striking differences that may have processing consequences. For example, sentences containing relative clauses with covert anaphors often appear to offer clues that they represent processing exceptions; they may have noncanonical word order in that they contain apparently objectless verbs (i.e., they contain gaps), and they will often contain relative pronouns (in French and other Romance languages, the relative pronoun is in fact obligatory). Either or both of these features could serve as signals to the parser that the structure being parsed contains a displaced item that will have a trace. On the other hand, with declarative French sentences containing raised lexical verbs, there are no such clues, probably because none are needed: since lexical verb raising does not lead to noncanonical word order, no gaps result. Sentences such as 6.5 thus seem to offer the possibility of a strong test of the trace reactivation account; if participants do turn out to be measurably sensitive to traces in such sentences, they will have shown said sensitivity in the absence of clues such as gaps and relative pronouns that have often been present in sentences used in previous studies.

Also, because of the nature of the structure tested, while support for the trace reactivation account can come from a positive result, that is, from priming effects at a trace point, and evidence against the account can come from a negative result at the same trace point, support for the direct association hypothesis can only come from a negative result, that is, from the absence of a priming effect at the same trace point. My stance on this design feature of the sentence-level verb experiment is that while a design allowing for both positive and negative findings for all hypotheses is always preferable, in this instance it was simply not possible. This is because the direct association hypothesis is concerned with the association of objects with their subcategorizer, not with the association of an overt subcategorizer with a point in the sentence where that subcategorizer was "originally" before being displaced. Indeed, no traces of any kind play a processing role in the direct association hypothesis. Therefore, if no priming effects with a subcategorizer are found at a point in a sentence where generative syntactic theory argues that there should be a trace, then in the context of our discussion, this negative result can only constitute partial support of the direct association hypothesis. The structure tested does of course allow for a full test of the trace reactivation account; therefore, results will be reported in terms of this model, with the understanding that if the trace reactivation account is found wanting, that finding also constitutes partial support, or circumstantial evidence, in favor of the direct association hypothesis. Even with interpretable results, findings will need to be replicated with other languages having obligatory lexical verb raising. The sentence-level verb study should therefore be seen in its proper light: as a motivated but preliminary attempt to use a displaced element other than a noun as a way of distinguishing between competing sentence-processing theories.

Experiment 4: Syntactic Priming of French Verbs

This experiment was designed to investigate whether French verbs can be primed by the syntactic structure of the utterances in which they appear. Of particular interest in this study is the interaction between verb movement (specifically, lexical verb raising) and verb inflectional morphology. The amount of syntactic priming was compared between inflected verbs and their base forms, together with word and nonword control conditions.

In French sentences such as 6.6, which contain finite lexical verbs followed by adverbs, the finite French lexical verb *conduisent* appears to the left of the adverb *illégalement,* in contrast to English, where the verb appears to the right of the adverb *(cf. the mechanics are illegally driving / *driving illegally the cars of their customers).*

> **6.6** *Les garagistes conduisent illégalement les voitures de leurs clients.*

Together with other contrasting distributional evidence from French and English concerning verb-negation order, infinitive-adverb word orders, and the possibility of question formation through subject–lexical verb inversion, Pollock (1989) argued that the contrasting finite verb-adverb orders of English and French reflects the fact that in French, but not in English, finite lexical verbs obligatorily raise, that is move leftward in a sentence, from VP (verb phrase) to INFL (inflectional phrase). Moreover, Pollock suggested that the verb-negation and verb-adverb orders of French, the possibility of question formation through inversion in French, and distributional facts of French infinitives with respect to negation and adverbs could all be explained through assuming a split INFL. Specifically, Pollock proposed that INFL consisted of two functional phrases, TP (tense phrase) and AgrP (agreement phrase), with TP occupying a higher structural position (meaning a more leftward position) than AgrP. Leaving out certain details not relevant to the discussion, according to Pollock's analysis French finite lexical verbs such as *conduisent* obligatorily raise from V (the head of VP) to T (the head of TP), leaving behind a phonetically null but syntactically active trace in V. In English, however, finite lexical verbs do not raise, but instead remain within VP. Thus, there are no traces associated with English finite lexical verbs (for more precise details concerning the arguments for the split-INFL hypothesis, see Pollock, 1989).

More recent theoretical perspectives exist of this contrast between French and English (cf. Chomsky, 1995). What is important for the present discussion is that according to both Pollock's analysis and later ones, the claim that French finite lexical verbs overtly raise while English finite lexical verbs do not is unchanged.

Given that they are said to contain raised verbs, sentences such as 6.5 and 6.6 appear to offer an opportunity to investigate the relation between a syntactic process (i.e., lexical verb raising) and a morphological process (i.e., verb inflection). On the assumption that, as in the previous sentence-level study with *wh*-moved nouns, the raising account of verbs will also turn out to have processing relevance, sentences such as 6.5 and 6.6 will be used in the present study, which will investigate the processing of French inflectional morphology in the context of sentences. That is, the study will address the interaction between syntactic and morphological knowledge within a processing context.

As with the previous sentence-level experiment, the basic experimental design was modeled upon that used by Swinney et al. (1988). Auditory primes consisted of French sentences containing raised regular and irregular verbs. Visually presented targets related to the regular and irregular raised verbs were presented at three different points during the playback of a carrier sentence: before, at, and after the location of a trace point. The present studies again used targets that were morphologically related to moved elements; whereas before, the relation concerned derivational morphology, in the present study we examined inflectional morphology.

Sentence 6.6 is repeated below as sentence 6.7 for reference.

6.7 *Les garagistes conduisent $_i$ illégalement t $_i$ les voitures de leurs clients.*

Given auditorily presented sentences such as 6.7, in which either a regular or an irregular verb has been raised (in sentence 6.7, the verb *conduisent* is irregular), presumably leaving behind a phonetically empty, syntactically active trace in its original location within VP, and given visually presented targets that are either identical to (e.g., *conduisent*) or morphologically related to (e.g., *conduire*) raised verbs, or are unrelated control words matched for length and frequency to the identical target condition (e.g., *appelaient*), French participants should show a significant interaction between the syntactic position corresponding to the target's presentation (i.e., pre-trace, trace, or post-trace point) and the target's morphological features. Specifically, with both regular and irregular verbs, participants should make faster lexical decisions at trace and post-trace points to both identical and morphologically related visual targets. Furthemore, RTs to lexical decisions should be faster at the trace point than at the earlier pre-trace point, though RTs to identical and morphologically related visual targets at the trace point should not themselves differ statistically. This pattern of results would suggest that as in the word-level verb study, the French participants were again demonstrating a sensitivity to the morphological structure of French verbs, but this time through priming from inaudible, syntactically active traces. Such results would also suggest that

for French participants, syntactic knowledge and morphological knowledge influence each other during sentence processing.

METHOD
Participants

Thirty-two French native speakers (age range 26–41, mean =
32), all with normal or corrected vision and with no reported
hearing abnormalities, participated in the experiment.

Stimuli

Twenty-one test sentences, all declaratives such as sentence 6.8,
with finite, transitive main verbs and raised lexical verbs, were
created for this experiment (the complete list of sentences can
be found in the appendix).

> **6.8** *Les gendarmes révèlent que les garagistes con-*
> *duisent* $_i$ *illégalement et pratiquement tous les soirs t* $_i$
> *les voitures de leurs clients.*

The main-clause verb was added in order to have a raising-
verb control condition (to be explained below). In order to
avoid the effects of repetition priming arising from too close
an overlap between the auditory primes and visual stimuli, it
was decided to use somewhat longer adverb phrases between
the raised verbs and their following objects. The sentences
contained an average of 16.6 words each (range approximately
15–19 words). As in the previous experiment, a female French
native speaker was digitally recorded (sampling rate 22050 Hz;
16-bit quantization; in stereo) while reading the sentences at a
normal rate of speaking. The average duration of the test sentences was 6.1 seconds. Using a sound editor, cursors were placed

into the resulting sound files at three different locations: within the middle of the second of the conjoined adverbial phrases, immediately following the second of the conjoined adverbial phrases but before the direct object of the raised verb (this corresponded to the trace position), and within the phrase modifying the direct object of the raised verb. These cursors served as prompts for displaying one of four types of visual targets during the audio playback of a sentence: identical targets (e.g., *conduisent*), morphologically related targets (e.g., *conduire*), frequency- or length-matched control targets (e.g., *appelaient*), and nonce targets (e.g., **bidocre*). The resulting design included twenty-one test sentences times four kinds of visual stimuli times three points of appearance, for a total of 252 trials. To have an equal number of real- and nonce-word trials, an additional forty-two distracter sentences were created. These were similar in structure to the test items but with nonce-word targets appearing at three different places during audio playback, for a total of 126 additional nonce-word trials. The final number of trials included 189 real-word trials and 189 nonce-word trials, for a total of 378 trials.

In order to have a baseline condition from which to measure the effects of syntactic priming, a set of control items was created from the test sentences. Each test sentence began with a main-clause verb that had not raised from within the subordinate clause (e.g., *révèlent,* from sentence 6.8 above); in the control condition, visual targets related to these verbs replaced the targets related to the raised verbs of the subordinate clauses. For this second set of items, the same three syntactically defined cursor points (pre-trace, trace, and post-trace) were used to display one of three kinds of visual targets: an identical target (e.g., *révèlent*), a morphologically related target (e.g., *révéler*), a frequency- or length-matched control target (e.g., *poussent*), and a nonce target (e.g., **kelsent*). The resulting baseline items included twenty-one test sentences times four types of visual targets times three points of target appearance, for a total of 252 trials, of which sixty-three were nonceword trials. To balance the number of real- and nonce-word trials among the control items, an additional forty-two distracter sentences were created. These were similar in structure to the test items but with nonce-word targets appearing at three different places during audio playback, for a total of 126 additional nonce-word trials. The final number of control trials included 189 real-word trials and 189 nonce-word trials, for a total of 378 control trials.

In order to prevent subjects from being presented with the same sentence twice, items were counterbalanced across visual-target type, visual-target position, and syntactic-priming condition. This resulted in the creation of twenty-four different experimental lists. Twelve of the lists consisted of sentences containing raised lexical verbs; the remaining twelve lists consisted of sentences containing nonraised lexical verbs. Twenty participants were tested on the sentences containing raised lexical verbs, while twelve participants were tested on the baseline sentences.

PROCEDURE

Subjects were tested individually in a quiet room. Written instructions specified that subjects were to listen to short French sentences playing over their headphones, and that at different moments during a sentence's playback, a string of letters would appear at the center of their computer screen (marked with two crosses: ++). The instructions specified that while some letter strings would be legitimate French words (e.g., *man-*

gent), others would not be (e.g., **flensent*), and that upon the appearance of each string the subject was to decide as quickly as possible whether it constituted a legitimate French word. The instructions emphasized both speed and accuracy in responding.

Trials began with a five-hundred-millisecond pause, followed by the display of a focus point at the center of the computer screen (++). Following another five-hundred-millisecond pause, a sentence began playing over the subject's headphones. When a cursor was reached in a given sound file, the focus point was replaced by a target word, which appeared on screen for one second or until the subject pressed a response button.

RESULTS

RTs greater than 1,500 milliseconds were discarded. This resulted in a loss of 2.1 percent of the data. Errors constituted 6 percent of the data, occurring primarily with critical sentences in the pre-trace condition; these were also removed from the data prior to analysis. As before, to reduce skew while retaining numerical outliers, RTs were inversely transformed prior to statistical analysis. ANOVAs examining the factor of list for raised and baseline sentences failed to reveal an effect of list for either set of sentences; therefore, within each condition (raised vs. baseline), results from all lists were pooled.

The degree of priming and evidence of trace reactivation were determined following the same method as in the previous sentence-level experiment with *isme*- and *té*-suffixed nouns. For each point at which a target was visually presented (i.e., at pre-trace, trace, and post-trace points) during the auditory playback of a sentence, an ANOVA was run on the RTs to identical, morphologically related, and control targets that were presented at that point. Significant priming was claimed in cases where for a given point, there were significant differences between RTs to identical versus control targets or between RTs to morphological versus control targets. Evidence of trace reactivation was claimed when there was significant priming at a point predicted to contain a silent, syntactically active trace by the trace reactivation account.

Findings: Raised Regular and Irregular Verbs

For reference, sentence 6.8 above is repeated as sentence 6.9 here.

> **6.9** Les gendarmes révèlent que les garagistes conduisent $_i$ illégalement et pratiquement tous les soirs t $_i$ les voitures de leurs clients.

An initial ANOVA with the within-subjects factor of regularity (regular vs. irregular verbs) failed to reveal a significant difference in RT ($p = .17$). Following this, a second ANOVA was run with the between-subjects factor of list. As these analyses failed to reveal significant list or regularity effects, all lists and all regular and irregular verbs were combined for the analyses described below.

Table 6.1 charts the mean RTs by target type (identical, morphologically related, and control) for targets related to both regular and irregular raised verbs at the pre-trace point. The ANOVA run on these RTs just missed significance ($F(2, 15) = 2.6, p = .08$).[19]

Table 6.2 charts the mean RTs by target type for targets related to both regular and irregular verbs at the trace point. The ANOVA for these RTs revealed a significant difference ($F(2, 19) = 9.6, p = .0004$). Planned comparisons revealed that while the eighteen-millisecond RT difference between identi-

Table 6.1. Means table for pre-trace point; raised regular and irregular verbs

	Count	Mean RT	Std. Dev.	Std. Err.
Control	16	807	134.8	33.7
Identical	16	759	172.4	43.1
Morphological	16	697	127.3	31.8

cal and morphologically related targets was not significant, both the 177-millisecond control-identical difference and the 159-millisecond control-morphological difference were significant (t (19) = 3.8, p = .001, and t (19) = 3.2, p = .004, respectively).

Table 6.3 charts the mean RTs by target type for targets related to both regular and irregular verbs at the post-trace point. An ANOVA revealed that RT differences at the post-trace point were significant (F (2, 19) = 6.02, p = .005). Planned comparisons revealed that while the RT difference between identical and morphologically related targets was not significant, the 130-millisecond RT difference between control and identical targets and the 95-millisecond RT difference between control and morphologically related targets were both significant (t (19) = 3.1, p = .005, and t (19) = 2.2, p = .03, respectively).

Table 6.2. Means table for trace point; raised regular and irregular verbs

	Count	Mean RT	Std. Dev.	Std. Err.
Control	20	871	229.9	51.4
Identical	20	694	161.1	36
Morphological	20	712	128.2	28.6

Table 6.3. Means table for post-trace point; raised regular and irregular verbs

	Count	Mean RT	Std. Dev.	Std. Err.
Control	20	801	154.9	34.6
Identical	20	671	109.7	24.5
Morphological	20	706	133.7	29.9

The results with regular and irregular verbs are summarized in table 6.4 below. From this presentation of the results, we can see that there is significant priming at the trace point for both identical and morphologically related targets. Furthermore, there is evidence of continued activation even at the post-trace point. This means that in accordance with the predictions of the trace reactivation account, there was reactivation at the trace point. Also, in accordance with words and rules theory, and in line with our predictions regarding trace

Table 6.4. Priming advantage (lexical-decision RTs to control words minus RTs to test words, in milliseconds) for identical and morphologically related targets at each visual probe point; all critical regular and irregular verbs

	Visual probe point		
	Pre-trace	Trace	Post-trace
Identical targets	48	177**	130**
Morphologically related targets	110	159**	95*

* $p < .05$
** $p < .01$

reactivation in the case of morphologically decomposable items, there was equally strong priming with both regular and irregular verbs and with both identical and morphologically related targets.

Findings: Baseline Condition Sentences

Finally, we turn to the analysis of the baseline sentences. For reference, sentence 6.9 above is repeated as sentence 6.10 here.

> **6.10** *Les gendarmes révèlent que les garagistes conduisent $_i$ illégalement et pratiquement tous les soirs t $_i$ les voitures de leurs clients.*

Compared to the critical sentences, there was a relatively greater percentage of errors (11 percent) among the baseline sentences, with the greatest proportion of errors occurring at the pre-trace point. As these sentences contained targets that were related to main-clause verbs such as *révèlent,* but were displayed at points in the sentence related to subordinate-clause verbs such as *conduisent,* no patterns of trace reactivation were anticipated. This is the result I observed: in contrast to the critical sentences, the baseline sentences failed to reveal significant RT differences at the trace point. In fact, there were no significant differences in RT for any of the three points at which targets were presented. Table 6.5 presents the RTs by target type for targets related to main-clause verbs at the pre-trace, trace, and post-trace points.

Conclusion

Table 6.6 presents the results by target position for the baseline sentences. Comparison of table 6.6 with table 6.4 reveals that

Table 6.5. RTs by target type for targets related to main-clause verbs at the pre-trace, trace, and post-trace points

	Count	Mean RT	Std. Dev.	Std. Err.
ANOVA and means table for RTs to targets in baseline sentences; pre-trace point : $F(2, 9) = 1.3$, $p = .3$				
Control	10	808	181.3	57.3
Identical	10	755	160.6	50.8
Morphological	10	713	127.4	40.3
ANOVA and means table for RTs to targets in baseline sentences; trace point: $F(2, 11) = .6$, $p = .5$				
Control	12	862	164.6	47.5
Identical	12	803	167	48.2
Morphological	12	833	142.1	41
ANOVA and means table for RTs to targets in baseline sentences; post-trace point: $F(2, 11) = 1.9$, $p = .17$				
Control	12	906	267.5	77.2
Identical	12	807	188.6	54.4
Morphological	12	749	146.2	42.2

Table 6.6. Priming advantage (lexical-decision RTs to control words minus RTs to test words, in milliseconds) for identical and morphologically related targets at each visual probe point; all baseline (main-clause) verbs

	Visual probe point		
	Pre-trace	Trace	Post-trace
Identical targets	53	59	99
Morphologically related targets	95	29	157

in the case of the baseline sentences, there was no pattern of trace reactivation as there was with the critical sentences.

We now reexamine predictions 1–4, repeated below:

1. In a cross-modal lexical-decision experiment with auditorily presented French sentences containing finite lexical verbs that are thought to have obligatorily raised to the left of an adverb, and visually presented letter strings representing raised verbs, the trace reactivation account predicts that there should be priming in the form of faster lexical decisions to raised verbs at the hypothesized trace point than at other points in the sentence.

This prediction was confirmed; as we saw, there was evidence of trace reactivation with both regular and irregular verbs. This result suggests that traces resulting from raised lexical verbs are processed similarly to traces resulting from displaced nouns, and that both constructions can be accounted for through the trace reactivation account.

2. Given the same experimental paradigm, sentences, and stimuli, evidence of priming at the hypothesized trace point would be evidence against the direct association hypothesis.

This conclusion seems well supported. According to the direct association hypothesis, traces are irrelevant to processing. The present results suggest quite the opposite. To the extent that these findings were predicted by the trace reactivation account, they are to the same degree difficult to reconcile under the no-traces mechanism of the direct association hypothesis.

3. Given the same experimental paradigm, sentences, and stimuli, a dual-mechanism model such as words and rules theory predicts that priming should be observed when the visual stimulus at the trace point is either the raised verb itself or the verb's root form.

This conclusion also seems well supported. The findings suggest that similar to what had previously been observed in word-level priming experiments, inflected verbs in sentential contexts are also processed using rules.

4. Given the same experimental paradigm, sentences, and stimuli, trace reactivation with identical primes should be observed with both regular and irregular French verbs.

Given the evidence of both identical and morphological priming with regular and irregular inflected French verbs, this prediction, made with reference to our hypothesis that trace reactivation with identical primes would occur only when the antecedent was productively suffixed, also appears to have been confirmed.

In the next chapter, I will draw some conclusions regarding the findings of my experiments. I will also suggest possible avenues of future research.

Conclusion

In this chapter, I will review the findings of the four experiments. I will then consider the results of the experiments in light of the theories of lexical representation and sentence processing they were designed to test.

Experiment 1: Masked Priming with French Regular and Irregular Verbs

This experiment, a partial replication of the masked-priming study reported in Meunier and Marslen-Wilson, 2000, investigated whether an inflected French verb would prime its root form, and whether the priming effect would be dependent upon a verb's regularity. Degree of priming with regular and irregular verbs was also compared with an identical-priming condition and two control conditions.

Results suggested that for native French-speaking adults, inflected forms of French verbs were as effective as identical primes at priming their infinitival forms. However, in contrast to the results of English-based studies, both regular and irregular forms of inflected French verbs prime their infinitival forms better than length- and frequency-matched controls. What is more, regular and irregular verbs did not differ in the degree to which they primed their infinitival forms. Further findings from this experiment were that both third-person-plural and first-person-singular inflected verb forms were effective primes. However, first-person-plural inflected forms were not as effective at priming their infinitival forms as were third-person-singular inflected forms.

Experiment 2: Primed Lexical Decision with Derived French Nouns

In this experiment, I investigated whether a derived French noun would prime its root form, and whether the priming effect would be dependent upon the productivity of the derived noun's suffix. The amount of priming was compared between derived nouns with productive suffixes and their root forms, and derived nouns with less productive suffixes and their root forms. Degree of priming with productively and less productively suffixed nouns was also compared with an identical-priming condition and two control conditions.

Results indicated that with *isme*-suffixed French nouns, it was possible to statistically separate the effects of morphological from orthographic priming. However, with *té*-suffixed French nouns, it was not possible to separate morphological from orthographic priming. Given the dictionary and corpus evidence arguing against the productive status of the *-té* suffix, I suggested that participant responses in the morphological-priming condition with *té*-suffixed nouns were based not on derivational morphological relations between primes and stimuli, but on the form overlap shared by primes and stimuli in that condition.

Experiment 3: Syntactic Priming of French Nouns

This experiment was designed to investigate whether French nouns can be primed by the syntactic structure of the utterances in which they appear. Of particular interest in this study was the interaction between knowledge of noun movement (specifically, *wh*-traces) and knowledge of noun morphology. The amount of syntactic priming was compared between more productive and less productive derivationally suffixed nouns and their base forms, together with word and nonword control conditions. Specifically, participants made lexical decisions on visually presented stimuli while listening to French sentences that contained productively suffixed (*-isme*) and unproductively suffixed (*-té*) nouns that had undergone *wh*-movement; the visual stimuli appeared before, at, and after the hypothesized location of the *wh*-trace. There was also a baseline condition in which primes related to non-*wh*-moved nouns in the sentences appeared before, at, and after the hypothesized location of the trace of the *wh*-moved noun.

Results indicated a significant RT advantage with *isme*-suffixed nouns at the trace point for both identical and morphologically related targets versus control targets. Although with *isme*-suffixed nouns priming also occurred with morphologically related targets at the pre-trace point, the observed priming advantages were greater at the trace point than at the pre-trace point for both identical and morphologically related targets. No trace reactivation was observed with either identical or morphologically related targets for *té*-suffixed nouns. There was also no evidence of trace reactivation in the baseline sentences. This result seemed to suggest that in the case of *wh*-moved derived nouns, in order for identical priming to occur at trace positions, the antecedent of the trace should bear a productive suffix.

Experiment 4: Syntactic Priming of French Verbs

In this experiment, I attempted to see whether French verbs could be primed by the syntactic structure of the utterances in which they appeared. Of particular interest in this study was the interaction between verb movement (specifically, lexical verb raising) and verb inflectional morphology. The amount of syntactic priming was compared between inflected verbs and their base forms, and between word and nonword control conditions. As in the previous experiment, participants made lexical decisions on visually presented stimuli while listening to French sentences; however, in the present experiment, subordinate clauses contained tensed regular and irregular lexical verbs that, according to recent syntactic accounts (Pollock, 1989), obligatorily raise, leaving a trace in their original location. The visual stimuli appeared before, at, and after the hypothesized location of the trace. There was also a baseline condition in which primes related to main-clause verbs appeared before, at, and after the hypothesized location of the trace of the subordinate-clause verb.

Results indicated that there was evidence of trace reactivation with both regular and irregular verbs. There was no evidence of verb trace reactivation in the baseline sentences. This result suggested that traces resulting from raised lexical verbs are processed similarly to traces resulting from displaced nouns. Furthermore, this result seemed to confirm the hypothesis that in order for identical priming to occur at trace positions, the antecedent of the trace should bear a productive suffix.

Implications for Theories of Lexical Representation

Taken together, the findings of these four experiments support a theory of lexical representation in which the masked-priming patterns observed with inflected regular and irregular verbs, both of which are argued to be regularly (and productively) suffixed, and with productively suffixed nouns differ from the patterns observed with unproductively suffixed nouns. For these experiments, the pattern-association model of connectionism would predict varying degrees of widespread priming, presumably in accordance with the differing amounts of orthographic overlap present between virtually all items tested. We did observe effects of orthographic priming; while these effects were separable from priming effects with productively suffixed items, they were not separable from priming effects with unproductively suffixed items. Since morphological productivity has been argued to signal rule-based representations, the findings argue instead for a theory that posits both rule-based and non-rule-based (and presumably associatively based) lexical representations. In the present discussion, the theory that better predicts the observed behavior patterns is words and rules theory.

Implications for Theories of Sentence Processing

The results of the two sentence-level experiments support a theory of sentence processing in which silent, syntactically active traces from displaced nouns and verbs are of relevance to the parser. Of the three sentence-processing theories we considered (the competition model, the direct association hypothesis, and the trace reactivation account), only the trace reactivation account ascribes any importance to traces with respect to processing.

Implications of Priming Behaviors That Varied According to Priming Context and Item Productivity

Finally, recall that in our word-level noun study, with unproductively suffixed nouns we observed identical but not morphological priming (i.e., *propre* primed *propre,* but *propreté* did not prime *propre*), while in our sentence-level studies we observed no priming at *wh*-trace points at all with unproductively suffixed nouns. By contrast, we observed identical and morphological priming with productively suffixed nouns in both our word-level and our sentence-level studies (i.e., in both contexts *capital* primed *capital,* and *capitalisme* primed *capital*).

What is to be made of finding evidence of identical priming with *té*-suffixed nouns at the word level, but not at *wh*-trace points within sentences? One possible interpretation is that *wh*-trace reactivation, and presumably *wh*-movement, fails to occur at all with unproductively suffixed items. In my view, however, such an interpretation would be hasty; there is simply no other evidence to suggest that *wh*-constructions with productively suffixed nouns entail movement, while syntactically identical *wh*-constructions with unproductively suffixed nouns do not. Indeed, such a claim would appear to rest on the seeming impossibility of a syntactic difference (*wh*-movement vs. *wh*-in-situ; cf. Chang, 1997) arising from a difference in morphological productivity rather than from a difference in syntactic structure.

I posit instead that this result can be better understood by considering that the change from a word-level context to a sentence-level context may well have entailed a change from a context where orthographic-priming effects were measurable to a context in which they were far less measurable, if at all. Recall first that in the word-level experiment with unproductively suffixed nouns, we were unable to separate the effects of orthographic priming from the effects of morphological priming; our interpretation of that finding was that with unproductively suffixed nouns, orthographic-priming effects were what were actually being captured in the morphological-priming condition. Now, recall that traces are said to contain semantic and grammatical information pertaining to their antecedents. This implies that with appropriately designed stimuli, primed lexical decisions at trace points (i.e., reactivation effects) could be made on the basis of semantic and grammatical information (with grammatical information including, but not limited to, morphologically related information such as suffixal productivity) or, alternatively, on the basis of only one or the other kind of information. By contrast, orthographic information is not explicitly hypothesized to be available at the trace point. Moreover, orthographic representations should have played little or no role in a cross-modal priming experiment (i.e., the cross-modal priming technique is thought to privilege modality-neutral representations; for discussion, see Marslen-Wilson et al., 1994). Thus, with cross-modal syntactic priming we would in fact not expect to be able to design stimuli such that we would observe significant orthographically based reactivation effects. In the case of our sentence-level studies with regular and irregular verbs and productively suffixed nouns, reactivation very likely occurred on the basis of grammatical information (specifically, morphological information); as the stimuli were not designed on the basis of semantic overlap with antecedents, semantic information probably contributed far less to reactivation effects. In the case of unproductively suffixed nouns, however, neither morphological nor orthographic information was presumably available for reactivation. Semantic information pertaining to the antecedent could potentially have been available for reactivation; however, semantic information would not have strongly influenced lexical decision RTs since the stimuli for this experiment were not designed on the basis of associative or semantic antecedent-prime overlap.

Therefore, my view of the sentence-level results with unproductively suffixed nouns is that no trace-reactivation effects were observed because there were no suitable representations available to be reactivated by the visual stimuli. We would expect that in my experiments, the priming advantage with productively suffixed nouns, which I hold reflects use of morphological and possibly also semantic representations, is greater than what would have been observed if, for instance, stimuli had been designed to tap exclusively semantic information at the trace point. We could expect this on the assumption that tasks in which two kinds of information may be available will facilitate processing more readily than tasks in which only one kind of information, or no information at all, is available. I cannot find direct evidence to support this hypothesis from my sentence-level studies, since the stimuli in those studies were not designed to separately capture exclusively semantic versus morphological priming. However, Nicol and Swinney (1989) may offer tentative support for the idea that priming on the basis of semantic information alone would lead to attenuated priming effects relative to priming made on the basis of morphological and possibly semantic information. Numerous differences between their study and mine argue against direct comparisons; still, it is striking that the degree of the associatively (i.e., semantically) based trace reactivation that they observed (27 milliseconds) is several magnitudes smaller than the morphologically and possibly also semantically based effects I observed (approximately 150 milliseconds) with productively suffixed nouns.

Directions for Future Research

I will focus on two related avenues of possible future research. The first concerns the consistent finding throughout the four experiments that the historical and present-day distributional facts of suffixal productivity in French appear to have implications for the French native speaker's mental representation of lexicon and grammar. Given my findings with productively and unproductively derived nouns, I would expect that similar productivity contrasts with other French derivational suffixes would provoke priming patterns similar to those observed in our experiments. The same observations can be made concerning the findings of my sentence-level experiments; the results of both of the movement structures I examined were promising, however, only further research will determine whether other, similar structures (both in French and in other languages) lead to similar priming patterns.

A second possible avenue of future research concerns what the present studies, or ones like them, would reveal of the mental representation of lexicon and grammar in the second-language learner. In this regard, recent advancements in the field of cognitive neuroscience suggest that native and second-language speakers of French would behave differently when performing the word- and sentence-level experiments of this book. Michael Ullman's *declarative/procedural model* (see, e.g., Pinker and Ullman, 2002; Ullman, 2001a; 2001b) holds that the processing of simplex or idiosyncratic lexical items and grammar is linked to two separate memory systems within the brain. Together with memorized and other conscious forms of knowledge such as semantic and episodic knowledge, idiosyncratic lexical knowledge is part of the declarative-memory system; this system is itself part of a more general associative-memory system that is in part subserved by brain structures thought to underlie both the ability to form new memories and long-term memory capacity. Along with other implicit forms of knowledge, including skills or habits such as bicycle riding or game playing, grammatical knowledge is part of the procedural-memory system; this system is subserved largely by brain areas that are thought to have a prominent role in the learning, initiation, and coordination of simple and complex motor movements (for full details, see Ullman, 2001a; 2001b). In Ullman's view, the declarative-memory system mediates our ability to store and retrieve explicit (i.e., conscious), non-systematic, or otherwise idiosyncratic linguistic knowledge, while the procedural-memory system mediates our ability to perform implicit (i.e., unconscious) grammatical or other similarly symbolic computations that are characteristic of rule-based linguistic systems.

Intriguingly, Ullman also outlines a hypothesis concerning the locus of age-related decrements in one's ability to acquire and process a second language. Proposing that aging leads to impairment of the procedural-memory system for both first-language processing and second-language acquisition (in each case leading to a decreased ability to use grammar, while largely sparing the declarative-memory system and thus lexical abilities), Ullman suggests that second-language learners should show a greater dependency on the declarative-memory system in their use of both second-language grammar and lexicon. Put differently, grammatical and other symbolic processing carried out by procedural memory in first-language processing should tend to be carried out by declarative memory in second-language processing. According to Ullman, this age-related shift in favor of declarative memory should result in a second-language learner's tendency to store in the lexicon items normally computed by procedural memory in first-language processing. To the extent that the second-language lexicon has structured representations, however, some measure of productivity may still be observable for these stored items.

Finally, Ullman predicts that the second-language-learner shift to declarative memory will be mediated by both age of exposure and amount of exposure to the second language (i.e., practice). Ullman hypothesizes that as practice with the second language increases, so should the use of procedural memory for grammatical processing. Moreover, this trend should hold true even for learners with relatively advanced ages of exposure—meaning that with sufficient second-language use, late learners could come to rely less upon declarative memory (and presumably more upon procedural memory) to process grammar and other rule-based linguistic items.

My experiments appear to have tapped what could be characterized in the native speaker as declarative knowledge (in the form of unproductive morphology) and procedural knowledge (in the form of productive morphology and movement operations). If so, then with relatively inexperienced second-language speakers of French, the declarative/procedural hypothesis predicts that my experiments would reveal a rather different pattern of behavior than what was observed with French native speakers. Specifically, if symbolic processing carried out by procedural memory in first-language processing tends to be carried out by declarative memory in second-language processing, resulting in the storage and retrieval of items that would normally be computed by procedural memory in first-language processing, then with relatively inexperienced second-language speakers of French in word-level experiments like mine, we should not observe effects of morphological priming with inflected verbs or productively suffixed nouns. This would be because similar to what was observed with developmentally language-impaired (DLI) francophone Canadians in Royle, Jarema, and Kehayia, 2002, relatively inexperienced second-language speakers of French (or of any language) should also be morphologically "blind" (though of course for different reasons) to what for a French native speaker would be the internal morphological structure of the items tested. A foreseeable result of a word-level masked-priming experiment with relatively inexperienced second-language speakers of French would be for lexical-decision RTs for all items to vary in accordance with the surface frequency of the stimuli, with little or no discernible effects of morphologically conditioned priming. More complex and possibly more exciting results might be obtained at the sentence level. To the extent that RTs to lexical decisions at trace points were again seen to vary in accordance with the surface frequency of stimuli, and to the extent that priming effects failed to emerge at trace points, such results would be evidence for use of declarative rather than procedural knowledge in second-language grammatical processing. A final foreseeable result would be the gradual giving way, as a function of increasing second-language experience, of predominantly, or exclusively, associatively based responses in relatively inexperienced learners to more nativelike response patterns reflecting rule-based processing (i.e., procedural knowledge) with productively suffixed items and with movement operations.

Appendix

From experiment 1: Verbs taken from Royle, Jarema, and Kehayia, 2002, sorted according to regularity (regular, irregular)
and frequency (frequent, infrequent). Frequencies here and
throughout are the number of occurrences per million words
and were obtained online at http://www.lexique.org.

irregular, infrequent		irregular, frequent	
bénir	1.97	dire	784.10
braire	0.39	dormir	51.10
cuire	8.10	fuir	21.19
concevoir	18.61	mentir	9.97
déduire	8.39	rendre	128.35
fendre	4.13	perdre	70.39
atteindre	53.13	plaindre	14.65
conduire	34.32	plaire	12.68
médire	0.32	revenir	52.68
moudre	0.74	soutenir	18.45
pondre	1.13	tenir	104.52
teindre	0.87	vendre	23.03
tondre	0.77	vivre	138.97
tordre	2.90	vouloir	60.71

regular, infrequent		regular, frequent	
camper	3.03	baisser	9.68
farder	0.39	monter	57.71
fouiller	6.87	dîner	49.58
glousser	0.68	fâcher	2.39
jaser	0.48	louer	5.52
mâcher	2.06	pleurer	34.10
parier	2.32	plier	8.06
plisser	0.77	prier	13.26
ronfler	2.81	prouver	18.00
ronger	1.90	ranger	12.68
tester	0.94	réparer	9.58
trier	2.90	sonner	10.68
troquer	1.90	tarder	8.61
visser	0.55	tousser	3.13

From experiment 2: Nouns suffixed with *-isme* and *-té*, with their unsuffixed forms.

Noun	Root form	Noun	Root form
marxisme	marx	sainteté	saint
matérialisme	matériel	pauvreté	pauvre
socialisme	social	gaîté	gai
fanatisme	fanatique	chétiveté	chétif
productivisme	productif	gaucheté	gauche
baroquisme	baroque	brièveté	bref
capitalisme	capital	chasteté	chaste
patriotisme	patriote	souveraineté	souverain
symbolisme	symbole	fausseté	faux
ritualisme	rituel	joliveté	joli
féodalisme	féodal	moyenneté	moyen
neutralisme	neutre	lasciveté	lascif

From experiment 3: Twenty-five sentences containing displaced *isme*-suffixed nouns.

1. Le juge n'a pas pardonné le barbarisme que la foule sur la place a montré pendant la manifestation.
2. Les employés ont noté le favoritisme que les chefs de la compagnie combattent avec tant de véhémence.
3. Les visiteurs ont remarqué le dynamisme que le sculpteur de la grande école a insufflé à la statue.
4. Le professeur a compris le conformisme que les politiciens dans l'amphithéâtre ont adopté dans leur traité.
5. Le fermier a reconnu le commercialisme que le syndicat dans la région voulait dénoncer depuis un an.
6. Le général a apprécié le militarisme que les soldats de la milice ont montré pour l'inspection.
7. Les écoliers n'ont pas compris l'optimisme que l'instituteur dans le film a éprouvé envers ses étudiants.
8. L'empereur a condamné le sadisme que les mercenaires de l'autre armée lui ont infligé pendant la guerre.
9. Les spectateurs ont apprécié le surréalisme que le cinématographe de l'université a cultivé dans son film.
10. Le maire a applaudi l'urbanisme que l'architecte au bureau de commerce a manifesté dans ses manières.
11. Le prêtre n'a pas compris le fatalisme que les spectateurs à la célébration ont dénoncé pendant son serment.

12. Le proviseur a accepté l'idéalisme que les professeurs de son école ont montré dans leurs discussions.

13. L'infirmière n'a pas aimé l'infantilisme que le chirurgien de l'autre pavillon a révélé pendant la réunion.

14. L'ingénieur a pardonné l'individualisme que les ouvriers sous sa direction ont embrassé durant la cérémonie.

15. Le conducteur de taxi n'a pas apprécié l'égoïsme que le piéton dans le passage clouté a montré au carrefour.

16. Le chimiste n'a pas approuvé le mécanisme que l'assistant du laboratoire a utilisé pour obtenir les résultats.

17. Les producteurs ont acclamé le réalisme que l'animatrice dans leur studio a incorporé à ses dessins.

18. Les représentants n'ont pas compris le nationalisme que les résidents de la ville ont montré aux élections.

19. Le juge a soutenu le libéralisme que l'avocat dans la salle de tribunal a adopté pour la défense.

20. Le garde-forestier a rejeté le naturalisme que le campeur devant la cheminée a décrit pendant la randonnée.

21. Les chevaliers ont respecté l'impérialisme que le despote dans l'immense château prônait dans sa politique étrangère.

22. L'auteur n'a pas apprécié le snobisme que les lecteurs dans la bibliothèque ont affecté envers ses romans.

23. Le public n'a pas compris le criticisme que le chercheur du CNRS a tenté d'expliquer dans son discours.
24. Les spectateurs ont adoré l'illusionisme que le magicien au carnaval a incorporé dans ses tours.
25. Le chaman a reconnu le mythisme que les néophytes dans son village ont adopté dans leurs prières.

From experiment 3: Frequencies of displaced *isme*-suffixed nouns and corresponding length- and frequency-matched controls. Item numbers here correspond to the sentence numbers for *isme*-suffixed nouns above.

Noun	Frequency	Control	Frequency
1. barbarisme	.13	camionnage	.13
2. favoritisme	.35	disjoncteur	.35
3. dynamisme	6.90	richelieu	6.90
4. conformisme	4.19	prélèvement	4.19
5. commercialisme	0.00	bataillonnaire	0.00
6. militarisme	.19	pantouflage	.19
7. optimisme	6.32	châtiment	6.32
8. sadisme	1.35	baratin	1.35
9. surréalisme	5.71	compositeur	5.71
10. urbanisme	10	entourage	10
11. fatalisme	1.39	oligopole	1.39
12. idéalisme	3.19	fabricant	3.19
13. infantilisme	.61	conférencier	.61
14. individualisme	4.35	émerveillement	4.35
15. égoïsme	6.68	crochet	6.68
16. mécanisme	30.06	boulevard	30.06

Noun	Frequency	Control	Frequency
17. réalisme	11.29	visiteur	11.29
18. nationalisme	4.84	publicitaire	4.84
19. libéralisme	5.06	gémissement	5.06
20. naturalisme	1.81	martèlement	1.81
21. impérialisme	2.35	échauffement	2.35
22. snobisme	2.71	caniveau	2.71
23. criticisme	.26	hippocampe	.26
24. illusionisme	0.00	vociférateur	0.00
25. mythisme	0.00	voiturin	0.00

From experiment 3: Twenty-five sentences containing displaced *té*-suffixed nouns.

1. Le garde du corps a garanti la sureté que la star dans la limousine a exigée pendant le trajet.
2. Le restaurateur a applaudi la netteté que l'apprenti du boulanger a respectée dans son travail.
3. Le skipper a admiré l'habileté que les marins sur le paquebot de grande ligne ont déployée avec les voiles.
4. Le patron n'a pas apprécie la saleté que les invités du mariage ont laissée dans la salle de séjour.
5. L'inventeur a loué la légèreté que les chimistes de sa compagnie ont réussi à incorporer à leurs produits.
6. Le policier a souligné l'étrangeté que le suspect dans son comportement a affectée pendant l'interrogatoire.
7. Le professeur n'a pas aimé la grossièreté que l'étudiant dans la classe a défendue dans son argument.

8. Le curé a condamné la méchanceté que le parois-
sien dans sa haine a adoptée envers ses amis.

9. La mère a accepté la fermeté que le père dans son
attitude a montrée envers ses enfants.

10. Le médecin légiste a prélevé les impuretés que le
criminel dans sa hâte a laissées sur la table.

11. Le detective a remarqué la naïveté que le major-
dome de la victime a montrée dans sa réponse.

12. Le subordonnée a envié l'ancienneté que le supé-
rieur de l'autre service a mise en avant dans ses
remarques.

13. L'ouvrier a reçu la pelletée que son collègue avec
malice lui a balancée sur le dos.

14. La jeune femme a envié le decolleté que sa voisine
avec tant d'audace a harboré pour cette soirée.

15. Le voisin a mangé le feuilleté que le boulanger avec
son apprenti a confectionné avec tant de soin.

16. Le milliardaire a dénoncé l'oisiveté que sa fiancée
pendant toute la semaine a adoptée sur son yacht.

17. L'agresseur a ressenti l'âpreté que sa victime dans
sa rage lui a montrée en le poignardant avec le
couteau à pain.

18. Le chercheur a valorisé l'opiniâtreté que son assistant avec tant d'ardeur a maintenue pendant
toute l'expérience.

19. Le petit Pierre a admiré l'agileté que le trapéziste
avec assurance a déployée pendant son numéro.

20. L'acheteur a déploré la malhonnêteté que le gara-
giste sans vergogne a encouragée chez ses employés.

21. Le roi Léopold III a admiré l'entièreté que son
sujet sans arrière-pensée a adoptée dans son
opinion.

22. Le pasha a rejeté la citoyenneté que les envahisseurs dans leur mépris lui ont offerte à la fin de la guerre.
23. Le chirurgien a vérifié la pureté que le patient dans le bloc opératoire a exigée avant d'être opéré.
24. Le lieutenant a dénoncé la lâcheté que les soldats de son escouade ont montrée pendant la bataille.
25. Le criminel a remarqué la dureté que le juge dans la salle de tribunal a manifestée pendant le procès.

From experiment 3: Frequencies of displaced *té*-suffixed nouns and corresponding length- and frequency-matched controls. Item numbers here correspond to the sentence numbers for *té*-suffixed nouns above.

Noun	Frequency	Control	Frequency
1. sureté	0.00	typote	0.00
2. netteté	9.58	serrure	9.58
3. habileté	11.19	analogie	11.19
4. saleté	5.19	déesse	5.19
5. légèreté	9.55	centaine	9.55
6. étrangeté	4.71	chaudière	4.71
7. grossièreté	3.03	exagération	3.03
8. méchanceté	6.87	récréation	6.87
9. fermeté	7.26	musette	7.26
10. impuretés	2.61	ébénistes	2.61
11. naïveté	7.48	guitare	7.48
12. ancienneté	9.74	initiation	9.74
13. pelletée	0.00	méninge	0.00
14. décolleté	2.00	cadrature	2.00
15. feuilleté	1.58	rétention	1.58

Noun	Frequency	Control	Frequency
16. oisiveté	2.06	drôlerie	2.06
17. âpreté	2.42	étance	2.42
18. opiniâtreté	1.23	décrépitude	1.23
19. agileté	0.00	récence	0.00
20. malhonnêteté	1.10	chromosphère	1.10
21. entièreté	0.00	brocheuse	0.00
22. citoyenneté	.71	malfaisance	.71
23. pureté	15.71	ardeur	15.71
24. lâcheté	5.68	brûlure	5.68
25. dureté	10.26	mairie	10.26

From experiment 4: Twenty-one sentences containing main-clause (baseline) and subordinate-clause (critical) finite lexical verbs.

1. Les livres racontent qu'elles suivent rapidement et sans faire de bruit le chemin vers la forêt.
2. Jean et Flore admettent qu'ils boivent lentement et presque chaque matin le thé chaud de leur grand-mère.
3. Ils maintiennent que mes amis perdent complètement et totalement la tête quand ils voient ce mec.
4. Les notes indiquent qu'ils mangent régulièrement pendant la semaine des croissants au beurre.
5. Les témoins suggèrent qu'ils écoutent plutôt rarement pendant le semestre la radio dans la cuisine.
6. Les voisines constatent que les enfants embrassent affectueusement et avec beaucoup de tendresse Marie, leur bonne depuis dix ans.

7. Les véterinaires observent que Franck et Laurence promènent fréquemment et directement en face de l'école Gabriel, leur petit chien.

8. Les gendarmes révèlent que les garagistes conduisent illégalement et pratiquement tous les soirs les voitures de leurs clients.

9. Les étudiants remarquent que les artistes dessinent soigneusement pendant toute la discussion les descriptions du vieillard.

10. Les clients du restaurant notent que les serveurs nettoient nerveusement et pratiquement tous les soirs les couverts des motards.

11. Les garde-forestiers croient que les oiseaux picorent voracement pendant tout l'après-midi le millet dans la mangeoire.

12. Les inspecteurs d'académie rapportent que les instituteurs notent soigneusement et avec une tristesse profonde les copies de leurs étudiants.

13. Les architectes confirment que les ingénieurs discutent vivement pendant toute la réunion les plans des bâtiments.

14. Les professeurs voient que les étudiants copient soigneusement pendant tout la matinée les references aux articles.

15. Les usagers savent que les contrôleurs vendent pratiquement toujours pendant la semaine les billets de métro.

16. Les Dupont prétendent que les voisins prennent régulièrement et volontiers le bus pour aller chez ce boulanger.

17. Les assistants soutiennent que Paul et Robert finissent fréquemment pendant la semaine leurs devoirs avant la classe d'anglais.

18. Les chercheurs affirment que les techniciens découvrent quasiment chaque matin les solutions au problème.

19. Les voisins racontent que les charpentiers construisent rapidement et avec beaucoup d'adresse le garage de Mme. Duloc.

20. Les montmartrois constatent que Michèle et Laurence discernent clairement et complètement l'escalier qui leur était caché dans le brouillard.

21. Les Rothschild assurent que les jouaillers fondent lentement et avec beaucoup de soin leurs boucles d'oreille en or.

From experiment 4: Main-clause verbs, with their frequency values per million words and their frequency-matched controls. Values in parentheses indicate where a control word's frequency differed from a main-clause verb.

Verb	Frequency	Control
1. racontent	4.06	modifient
2. admettent	3.65	jouissent
3. maintiennent	3.48	répartissent
4. indiquent	4.58	emploient
5. suggèrent	2.97	échangent
6. constatent	1.35	empruntent
7. observent	3.97	déplacent
8. révèlent	8.52	poussent
9. remarquent	.74	sillonnent
10. notent	.52	fanent
11. observent	3.97	tendent (14.39)
12 rapportent	4.61	effectuent
13. confirment	3.03	remplacent

Verb	Frequency	Control
14. voient	18.9	aiment
15. savent	33.1	disent
16. prétendent	5.03	apparurent
17. soutiennent	3.71	répartissent
18. affirment	4.68	partagent
19. racontent	4.06	modifient
20. constatent	1.35	discernent (.45)
21. assurent	10.23	exercent

From experiment 4: Subordinate-clause verbs, with their frequency values per million words and their frequency-matched controls. Values in parentheses indicate where a control word's frequency differed from a subordinate-clause verb.

Verb	Frequency	Control
1. suivent	19.03	rendent (16.61)
2. boivent	3.61	coulent
3. perdent	9.52	sentent
4. mangent	5.23	dansent
5. écoutent	3.84	dressent (4)
6. embrassent	2.13	réagissent
7. promènent	2.16	associent
8. conduisent	9.9	appelaient
9. dessinent	4.1	racontent
10. nettoient	.58	prévalent
11. picorent	.26	énoncent
12. notent	.52	sèment
13. discutent	2.58	régissent
14. copient	.23	forgent
15. vendent	3.23	tentent

Verb	Frequency	Control
16. prennent	36.06	semblent
17. finissent	8.16	dépassent
18. découvrent	3.87	approchent
19. construisent	2.35	introduisent
20. observent	3.97	voient
21. fondent	4.42	roulent

Notes

1. Intelligent behavior in this context means "behavior that a human observer would classify as human or humanlike."

2. See, however, Norris, 1993, and Norris, McQueen, and Cutler, 2000, for arguments against the necessity of interactive networks.

3. While it appears to be true that children hear only correct rather than incorrect input, it does not appear that they consistently receive explicit negative evidence concerning the grammaticality of their productions (Brown and Hanlon, 1970). To the extent that this is true, the teacher function of the network may not be ecologically valid.

4. A suppletive form of a word is an inflected or derived form that has its origins in a totally different root. An example from English is *went,* the suppletive past-tense form of *go.* Etymologically, *went* is the past tense of *wend,* not of *go.*

5. This result also raises a question with respect to the findings with irregular French verbs: how do we reconcile the apparently contradictory results of the control participants with the unprimed and primed variants of the lexical-decision task? In the unprimed variant, as expected, irregulars provoked frequency effects, but in the primed variant they patterned like regulars in that priming was observed between irregular primes and targets. Given the findings of English and French studies that have used primed lexical-decision tasks, and given the morphological characteristics of French and English regular and irregular verbs, the answer I propose is that the two variants of the lexical-decision task are sensitive to different item characteristics, that is, the primed variant of the lexical-decision task is sensitive to morphological productivity in ways that the unprimed variant is not.

6. As no surface-frequency database exists for Canadian French, Royle, Jarema, and Kehayia (2002) sorted their items according to compound fre-

quency. There are, however, surface-frequency databases for European French, one of which (Lexique, available online at http://www.lexique.org) was consulted in order to verify that the relative compound-frequency values reported by the Royle team were roughly equivalent to the surface-frequency values for the same items in European French.

7. Of the priming studies outlined earlier (Kempley and Morton, 1982; Meunier and Marslen-Wilson, 2000; Napps, 1989; Orsolini and Marslen-Wilson, 1997; Royle, Jarema, and Kehayia, 2002; Stanners et al., 1979;), only Royle, Jarema, and Kehayia, 2002, controlled for both prime and stimulus frequency. This was due to their interest in testing the hypothesis that the SLI lexicon is "blind" to complex morphology (and thus blind to the difference between regular and irregular morphology) and is instead organized according to item frequency. None of the other studies, all of which (like the present study) examined pathological normals, controlled for either prime or stimulus frequency.

8. See also note 5 above.

9. The presentation of test items and recording of RTs for this and the three subsequent experiments reported here were controlled by IBM PC computers running DMDX, an experiment generator developed at Monash University and at the University of Arizona by K. I. Forster and J. C. Forster.

10. The use of counterbalancing in this experiment and in the ones that follow calls for regular F-ratios, that is, for standard subject analyses averaging over items (Raaijmakers, 2003; Raaijmakers, Schrijnemakers, and Gremm, 1999).

11. Owing to errors and to the use of a repeated design, three participants did not contribute data to every cell in this experiment; as a result, the reported degrees of freedom varied in certain analyses.

12. Not all theories of syntax assume the existence of traces. See Bresnan, 1982, and Pollard and Sag, 1994, for alternative accounts of *wh*-phenomena that do not hinge upon movement or traces.

13. Readers interested in the specifics of trace theory with reference to case marking in contractions should consult Chomsky, 1977, and Chomsky and Lasnik, 1978.

14. As noted by Nicol and Swinney (1989, pp. 8–9), the antecedent of the trace in sentence 6 is the relative pronoun *that* and not the head of the relative clause *boy*. Nicol and Swinney (1989) made the assumption that since the relative pronoun and the head of the relative are coreferential, the visual probes associated with *boy* should provoke antecedent priming effects.

15. There was no morphological-priming control condition due to the fact that it proved exceedingly difficult to devise semantically plausible sen-

tences with morphologically decomposable nouns. It was felt, however, that if no priming was observed with control nouns in the identical-priming condition, there would be little reason to expect morphological priming.

16. There were more participants than lists, which means that roughly half of the lists reflect responses from two participants rather than just one.

17. Owing to errors and to the use of a repeated design, two participants did not contribute data to every cell in this experiment; this accounts for the different reported degrees of freedom in certain analyses.

18. As there is no syntactic reason for priming to occur here, I will tentatively classify the pre-trace priming effects as a form of repetition priming.

19. Owing to errors (which in this case were concentrated in the pre-trace condition) and to the use of a repeated design, four participants did not contribute data to every cell; as a result, the reported degrees of freedom varied in certain analyses.

References

Anderson, J. (1983). A spreading activation theory of memory. *Journal of Verbal Learning and Verbal Behavior, 22,* 261–295.

Anisfeld, M. (1984). *Language development from birth to three.* Hillsdale, NJ: Lawrence Erlbaum Associates.

Anisfeld, M., and Tucker, G. R. (1967). English pluralization rules of six-year-old children. *Child Development, 38,* 1201–1217.

Anshen, F., and Aronoff, M. (1999). Using dictionaries to study the mental lexicon. *Brain and Language, 68,* 16–26.

Aronoff, M. (1976). *Word formation in generative grammar.* Cambridge, MA: MIT Press.

Baayen, H. (1992). Quantitative aspects of morphological productivity. *Yearbook of Morphology, 1991,* 109–149.

Baayen, H., and Lieber, R. (1991). Productivity and English word-formations: a corpus-based study. *Linguistics, 29,* 801–843.

Bates, E., and MacWhinney, B. (1982). Functionalist approaches to grammar. In E. Wanner and L. Gleitman (Eds.), *Language acquisition: The state of art* (pp. 173–217). New York: Cambridge University Press.

——— (1987). Competition, variation, and language learning. In B. MacWhinney (Ed.), *Mechanisms of language acquisition* (pp. 157–193). Mahwah, NJ: Lawrence Erlbaum Associates.

——— (1989). Functionalism and the competition model. In B. MacWhinney and E. Bates (Eds.), *The crosslinguistic study of sentence processing* (pp. 3–73). New York: Cambridge University Press.

Bauer, L. (2001). *Morphological productivity.* Cambridge: Cambridge University Press.

Berko, J. (1958). The child's learning of English morphology. *Word, 14,* 150–177.

Bresnan, J. (1982). *The mental representation of grammatical relations.* Cambridge, MA: MIT Press.

Brown, R. (1973). *A first language: The early stages.* Cambridge, MA: Harvard University Press.

Brown, R., and Hanlon, C. (1970). Derivational complexity and order of acquisition in child speech. In J. Hayes (Ed.), *Cognition and the development of language* (pp. 155–207). New York: Wiley.

Bryant, B., and Anisfeld, M. (1969). Feedback versus no feedback in testing children's knowledge of English pluralization rules. *Journal of Experimental Child Psychology, 8,* 250–255.

Bybee, J. L., and Modor, C. L. (1983). Morphological classes as natural categories. *Language, 59,* 251–271.

Bybee, J. L., and Slobin, D. I. (1982). Rules and schemas in the development and use of the English past tense. *Language, 58,* 265-289.

Chang, L. (1997). Wh-in situ phenomena in French. MA thesis, University of British Columbia.

Chomsky, N. (1977). On wh-movement. In P. Culicover, T. Wasow, and A. Akmajian (Eds.), *Formal syntax* (pp. 71–132). New York: Academic Press.

———— (1981). *Lectures on government and binding.* Foris: Dordrecht.

———— (1986). *Barriers.* Cambridge, MA: MIT Press.

———— (1995). *The minimalist program.* Cambridge, MA: MIT Press.

Chomsky, N., and Halle, M. (1968). *The sound pattern of English.* New York: Harper and Row.

Chomsky, N., and Lasnik, H. (1978). A remark on contraction. *Linguistic Inquiry, 9,* 268–274.

Clahsen, H. (1999). Lexical entries and rules of language: A multi-disciplinary study of German inflection. *Behavioral and Brain Sciences, 22,* 991–1013.

Clahsen, H., Eisenbeiss, S., Hadler, M., and Sonnenstuhl, I. (2001). The mental representation of inflected words: An experimental study of adjectives and verbs in German. *Language, 77 (3),* 510-543

Clahsen, H., Eisenbeiss, S., and Sonnenstuhl-Henning, I. (1997). Morphological structure and the processing of inflected words. *Theoretical Linguistics, 23,* 201–249.

Clahsen, H., and Featherston, S. (1999). Antecedent-priming at trace positions: Evidence from German scrambling. *Journal of Psycholinguistic Research, 28,* 415–437.

Clahsen, H., Sonnenstuhl, I., and Blevins, J. P. (2003). Derivational morphology in the German mental lexicon: A dual-mechanism account. In H. Baayen and R. Schreuder (Eds.), *Morphological structure in language processing* (pp. 125–155). Berlin: Mouton de Gruyter.

Collins, A. M., and Loftus, E. F. (1975). A spreading-activation theory of semantic processing. *Psychological Review, 82,* 407–428.

Drews, E. (1996). Morphological priming. *Language and Cognitive Processes, 11,* 629–634.

Dreyfus, H. L. (1992). *What computers still can't do: A critique of artificial reason.* Cambridge, MA: MIT Press.

Dubois, J. (1962). *Étude sur la dérivation suffixale en français moderne et contemporain; essai d'interprétation des mouvements observés dans le domaine de la morphologie des mots construits.* Paris: Larousse.

Dubois, J., and Dubois-Charlier, F. (1999). *La dérivation suffixale en français.* Paris: Nathan.

Dunlop, C. E. M., and Fetzer, J. H. (1993). *Glossary of cognitive science.* New York: Paragon House.

Elman, J. L., Bates, E. A., Johnson, M. H., Karmiloff-Smith, A., Parisi, D., and Plunkett, K. (1996). *Rethinking innateness: A connectionist perspective on development.* Cambridge, MA: Bradford Books.

Ervin, S. (1964). Imitation and structural change in children's language. In E. H. Lenneberg (Ed.), *New directions in the study of language* (pp. 163–189). Cambridge, MA: MIT Press.

Feustel, T. C., Shiffrin, R. M., and Salasoo, A. (1983). Episodic and lexical contributions to the repetition effect in word identification. *Journal of Experimental Psychology: General, 112,* 309–346.

Fodor, J. A. (1983). *The modularity of mind.* Cambridge, MA: MIT Press.

Forster, K. I. (1998). The pros and cons of masked priming. *Journal of Psycholinguistic Research, 27,* 203–233.

——— (1999). The microgenesis of priming effects in lexical access. *Brain and Language, 68,* 5–15.

Forster, K. I., and Davis, C. (1984). Repetition priming and frequency attenuation in lexical access. *Journal of Experimental Psychology: Learning, Memory, and Cognition, 10,* 680–698.

Fowler, C. A., Napps, S. E., and Feldman, L. B. (1985). Relations among regular and irregular morphologically related words in the lexicon as revealed by repetition priming. *Memory and Cognition, 13,* 241–255.

Frost, R., Forster, K. I., and Deutsch, A. (1997). What can we learn from the morphology of Hebrew? A masked-priming investigation of morphological representation. *Journal of Experimental Psychology: Learning, Memory, and Cognition, 23,* 829–856.

Gernsbacher, M. A. (1984). Resolving 20 years of inconsistent interactions between lexical familiarity and orthography, concreteness, and polysemy. *Journal of Experimental Psychology: General, 113,* 256–281.

Grainger, J., and Segui, J. (1990). Neighborhood frequency effects in visual word recognition: A comparison of lexical decision and masked identification latencies. *Perception & Psychophysics, 47,* 191–198.

Grainger, J., Colé, P., and Segui, J. (1991). Masked morphological priming in visual word recognition. *Journal of Memory and Language, 30,* 370–384.

Heilenman, L. K., and McDonald, J. L. (1993). Processing strategies in L2 learners of French: The role of transfer. *Language Learning, 43,* 507–557.

Jackendoff, R. S. (1975). Morphological and semantic regularities in the lexicon. *Language, 51,* 639–671.

Jacoby, L. L. (1983). Perceptual enhancement: Persistent effects of an experience. *Journal of Experimental Psychology: Learning, Memory, and Cognition, 9,* 21–38.

Johnson-Laird, P. N. (1988). *The computer and the mind.* Cambridge, MA: Harvard University Press.

Kempley, S. T., and Morton, J. (1982). The effects of priming with regularly and irregularly related words in auditory word recognition. *British Journal of Psychology, 73,* 441–454.

Kim, J., Pinker, S., Prince, A., and Prasada, S. (1991). Why no mere mortal has ever flown out to center field. *Cognitive Science, 15,* 173-218.

Kuczaj, S. A. (1977). The acquisition of regular and irregular past tense forms. *Journal of Verbal Learning and Behavior, 16,* 589–600.

Kuczaj, S. A. (1978). Children's judgments of grammatical and ungrammatical irregular past tense verbs. *Child Development, 49,* 319-326.

Longtin, C.-M., Segui, J., and Hallé, P. A. (2003). Morphological priming without morphological relationship. *Language and Cognitive Processes, 18,* 313–334.

MacWhinney, B. (1997). Second language acquisition and the competition model. In A. M. B. de Groot and J. F. Kroll (Eds.), *Tutorials in bilingualism: Psycholinguistic perspectives* (pp.113–144). Mahwah, NJ: Lawrence Erlbaum Associates.

——— (in press). A unified model of language acquisition. In J. F. Kroll and A. M. B. de Groot (Eds.), *Handbook of bilingualism: Psycholinguistic approaches.* New York: Oxford University Press.

MacWhinney, B., and Bates, E. (1978). Sentential devices for conveying givenness and newness: A cross-cultural developmental study. *Journal of Verbal Learning and Verbal Behavior, 17,* 539–558.

MacWhinney, B., and Leinbach, J. (1991). Implementations are not conceptualizations: Revising the verb learning model. *Cognition, 40,* 121–157.

Marcel, A. J. (1980). Conscious and preconscious recognition of polysemous words: Locating the selective effects of prior verbal context. In R. S. Nickerson (Ed.), *Attention and performance VIII* (pp. 435–457). Hillsdale, NJ: Lawrence Erlbaum Associates.

——— (1983). Conscious and unconscious perception: Experiments on visual masking and word recognition. *Cognitive Psychology, 15*, 197–237.

Marcus, G. F., Brinkman, U., Clahsen, H., Wiese, R., and Pinker, S. (1995). German inflection: The exception that proves the rule. *Cognitive Psychology, 29*, 189–256.

Marcus, G. F., Pinker, S., Ullman, M., Hollander, M., Rosen, T. J., and Xu, F. (1992). *Overregularization in language acquisition (Monographs of the Society for Research in Child Development), 57* (4, Serial No. 228).

Marslen-Wilson, W. D., Hare, M., and Older, L. (1993). Inflectional morphology and phonological regularity in the English mental lexicon. *Proceedings of the 15th Annual Conference of the Cognitive Science Society* (pp. 693–698). Hillsdale, NJ: Lawrence Erlbaum Associates.

——— (1995). Priming and blocking in the mental lexicon: The English past tense. Paper presented at the meeting of the Experimental Psychology Society, London.

Marslen-Wilson, W. D., and Tyler, L. (1998). Rules, representations, and the English past tense. *Trends in Cognitive Science, 2*, 428–435

Marslen-Wilson, W. D., Tyler, L., Waksler, R., and Older, L. (1994). Morphology and meaning in the English mental lexicon. *Psychological Review, 101*, 3–33.

Matthews, P. H. (1974). *Morphology.* Cambridge, UK: Cambridge University Press.

McClelland, J. L., and Elman, J. L. (1986). The TRACE model of speech perception. *Cognitive Psychology, 18*, 1–86.

McClelland, J. L., and Patterson, K. (2002). Rules or connections in past tense inflections: What does the evidence rule out? *Trends in Cognitive Sciences, 6* (11), 465–472.

McKoon, G., and Ratcliff, R. (1992). Spreading activation versus compound cue accounts of priming: Mediated priming revisited. *Journal of Experimental Psychology: Learning, Memory, and Cognition, 18* (6), 1155–1172.

Meunier, F., and Marslen-Wilson, W. D. (2000). Regularity and irregularity in French inflectional morphology. *Proceedings of the 22nd Annual Meeting of the Cognitive Science Society* (pp. 346–351). Mahwah, NJ: Lawrence Erlbaum Associates.

Meunier, F., and Marslen-Wilson, W. D. (2004). Regularity and irregularity in French verbal inflection. *Language and Cognitive Processes, 19* (4), 561–580.

Meyer, D. E., and Schvaneveldt, R. W. (1971). Facilitation in recognizing pairs of words: Evidence of a dependence between retrieval operations. *Journal of Experimental Psychology, 90,* 227–234.

Minsky, M. (1975). A framework for representing knowledge. In P. Winston (Ed.), *The psychology of computer vision* (pp. 211–277). New York: McGraw-Hill.

Murrell, G. A., and Morton, J. (1974). Word recognition and morphemic structure. *Journal of Experimental Psychology, 102,* 963–968.

Nakano, Y., Felser, C., and Clahsen, H. (2002). Antecedent priming at trace positions in Japanese long-distance scrambling. *Journal of Psycholinguistic Research, 31,* 531–571.

Napps, S. E. (1989). Morphemic relationships in the lexicon: Are they distinct from semantic and formal relationships? *Memory and Cognition, 17,* 729–739.

Neely, J. H. (1977). Semantic priming and retrieval from lexical memory: Evidence for facilitatory and inhibitory processes. *Journal of Experimental Psychology: General, 3,* 226–254.

Newell, A. (1980). Physical symbol systems. *Cognitive Science, 4,* 135–183.

Newell, A., and Simon, H.A. (1972). *Human problem solving.* Englewood Cliffs, NJ: Prentice Hall.

Nicol, J. (1988). Coreference processing during sentence comprehension. PhD dissertation, Massachusetts Institute of Technology.

——— (1993). Reconsidering reactivation. In G. T. M. Altmann and R. Shillcock (Eds.), *Cognitive models of speech processing: The second Sperlonga meeting* (pp. 321–350). Hillsdale, NJ: Lawrence Erlbaum Associates.

Nicol, J., Fodor, J. D., Swinney, D. (1994). Using cross-modal lexical decision tasks to investigate sentence processing. *Journal of Experimental Psychology: Learning, Memory, and Cognition, 20,* 1229–1238.

Nicol, J., and Swinney, D. (1989). The role of structure in coreference assignment during sentence processing. *Journal of Psycholinguistic Research, 18,* 5–19.

Norris, D. G. (1993). Bottom-up connectionist models of 'interaction.' In G. T. M. Altmann and R. Shillcock (Eds.), *Cognitive models of speech processing: The second Sperlonga meeting* (p. 211–234). Hillsdale, NJ: Lawrence Erlbaum Associates.

Norris, D. G., McQueen, J. M., and Cutler, A. (2000). Merging information in speech recognition: Feedback is never necessary. *Behavioral and Brain Sciences, 23* (3), 299–325.

Orsolini, M., and Marslen-Wilson, W. D. (1997). Universals in morphological representation: Evidence from Italian. *Language and Cognitive Processes,* 12, 1–47.

Pakkenberg, B., and Gundersen, H. J. G. (1997). Neocortical neuron number in humans: Effect of sex and age. *Journal of Comparative Neurology, 384,* 312–20.

Pakkenberg, B., Pelvig, D., Marner, L., Bundgaard, M. J., Gundersen, H. J. G., Nyengaard, J. R., and Regeur, L. (2003). Aging and the human neocortex. *Experimental Gerontology, 38,* 95–99.

Pickering, M., and Barry, G. (1991). Sentence processing without empty categories. *Language and Cognitive Processes, 6,* 229–259.

Pinker, S. (1991). Rules of language. *Science, 253,* 530–535.

Pinker, S. (2000). *Words and rules: The ingredients of language.* New York: Perennial.

Pinker, S., and Prince, A. S. (1988). On language and connectionism: Analysis of a parallel distributed processing model of language acquisition. *Cognition, 28,* 73–193.

——— (1991). Regular and irregular morphology and the psychological status of rules of grammar. In S. D. Lima, R. L. Corrigan, and G. K. Iverson (Eds.), *The reality of linguistic rules* (pp. 321–350). Amsterdam: John Benjamins.

Pinker, S., and Ullman, M. (2002). The past and future of the past tense. *Trends in Cognitive Sciences, 6* (11), 456–463.

Plunkett, K., and Marchman, V. (1993). From rote learning to system building: Acquiring verb morphology in children and connectionist nets. *Cognition, 48,* 21–69.

Pollard, C., and Sag, I. A. (1994). *Head-driven phrase structure grammar.* Chicago: University of Chicago Press.

Pollock, J.-Y. (1989). Verb movement, universal grammar and the structure of IP. *Linguistic Inquiry, 20,* 365–424.

Prasada, S., and Pinker, S. (1993). Generalisation of regular and irregular morphological processes. *Language and Cognitive Processes, 8,* 1–56.

Pylyshyn, Z.W. (1984). *Computation and cognition.* Cambridge, MA: MIT Press.

Raaijmakers, J. G. W. (2003). A further look at the "language-as-fixed-effect fallacy." *Canadian Journal of Experimental Psychology, 57,* 141–151.

Raaijmakers, J. G. W., Schrijnemakers, J. M. C., and Gremm, F. (1999). How to deal with "the language-as-fixed-effect fallacy": Common misconceptions and alternative solutions. *Journal of Memory and Language, 41,* 416–426.

Rajaram, S., and Neely, J.H. (1992). Dissociative masked repetition priming and word frequency effects in lexical decision and episodic recognition tasks. *Journal of Memory and Language, 31,* 152–182.

Ratcliff, R. (1993). Methods for dealing with outliers. *Psychological Review, 114,* 510–532.

Ratcliff, R., and McKoon, G. (1988). A retrieval theory of priming in memory. *Psychological Review, 95,* 385–408.

———. (1994). Retrieving information from memory: Spreading-activation theories versus compound-cue theories. *Psychological Review, 101,* 177–184.

Royle, P., Jarema, G., and Kehayia, E. (2002). Frequency effects on visual word access in developmental language impairment. *Journal of Neurolinguistics, 15,* 11–41.

Rumelhart, D. E., and McClelland, J. L. (1986). On learning the past tenses of English verbs. In Rumelhart, D. E., McClelland, J. L., and PDP Research Group, Eds., *Parallel distributed processing: Explorations in the microstructure of cognition. Volume 2: Psychological and biological models* (pp. 216–271). Cambridge, MA: MIT Press.

Rumelhart, D. E., McClelland, J. L., and PDP Research Group, Eds. (1986). *Parallel distributed processing: Explorations in the microstructure of cognition. Volume 1: Foundations.* Cambridge, MA: MIT Press.

Schank, R. C., and Abelson, R. P. (1977). *Scripts, plans, goals, and understanding: An inquiry into human knowledge structures.* Hillsdale, NJ: Lawrence Erlbaum Associates.

Sereno, J. A. (1991). Graphemic, associative, and syntactic priming effects at brief stimulus onset asynchrony in lexical decision and naming. *Journal of Experimental Psychology: Learning, Memory, and Cognition, 17,* 459–477.

Shallice, T. (1988). *From neuropsychology to mental structure.* Cambridge, UK: Cambridge University Press.

Slobin, D. I., Ed. (1985). *The crosslinguistic study of language acquisition* (Vols. 1–2). Hillsdale, NJ: Lawrence Erlbaum Associates.

Sonnenstuhl, I., Eisenbeiss, S., and Clahsen, H. (1999). Morphological priming in the German mental lexicon. *Cognition, 72,* 203–236.

Stanners, R. F., Neiser, J. J., Hernon, W. P., and Hall, R. (1979). Memory representation for morphologically related words. *Journal of Verbal Learning and Verbal Behavior, 18,* 399–412.

Swinney, D., Ford, M., Frauenfelder, U., and Bresnan, J. (1988). On the temporal course of gap-filling and antecedent-assignment during sentence processing. In Grosz, B., Kaplan, R., Macken, M., and Sag, I., Eds., *Lan-*

guage Structure and Processing. Stanford, CA: Center for the Study of Language and Information.

Swinney, D., Onifer, W., Prather, P., and Hirshkowitz, M. (1979). Semantic facilitation across sensory modalities in the processing of individual words and sentences. *Memory and Cognition, 7,* 159–165.

Tabossi, P. (1996). Cross-modal semantic priming. *Language and Cognitive Processes, 11,* 569–576.

Thiele, J. (1987). *La formation des mots en français moderne.* Montréal: Les Presses de l'Université de Montréal.

Ullman, M. T. (2001a). The declarative/procedural model of lexicon and grammar. *Journal of Psycholinguistic Research, 30,* 37–69.

——— (2001b). The neural basis of lexicon and grammar in first and second language: The declarative/procedural model. *Bilingualism: Language and Cognition, 4,* 105–122.

Winograd, T. (1970). Procedures as a representation for data in a computer program for understanding natural language. PhD dissertation, Massachusetts Institute of Technology.

Index